D0909012

ALSO BY G. WAYNE MILLER

FICTION

Thunder Rise

NONFICTION

The Work of Human Hands

Coming of Age

COMING OF AGE

*The True Adventures of
Two American Teens*

G. WAYNE MILLER

RANDOM HOUSE • NEW YORK

Portions of this work were originally published in
The Providence Journal-Bulletin in different form.

Library of Congress Cataloging-in-Publication Data
Miller, G. Wayne.
Coming of age / G. Wayne Miller.
p.   cm.
ISBN 0-679-42326-5
1. Teenagers—Rhode Island—Social conditions—Case studies.
2. High school students—Rhode Island—Case studies.   I. Title.
HQ796.M484   1995
305.23′5′0973—dc20   94-20307

Manufactured in the United States of America
24689753
First Edition

*With profound appreciation to
my parents, Roger and Mary Miller,
who always helped me toward my dreams*

Contents

AUTHOR'S NOTE   *xi*
INTRODUCTION   *xiii*

FALL

1. *TOTAL GODHEAD*   *3*
2. DROUIN   *13*
3. STARS   *25*
4. HAIRY GNOME SCROTUMS   *39*
5. BETH   *61*
6. THE TURTLE INCIDENT   *83*

WINTER

7. BRONCOS   *97*
8. WICKED SWEDISH   *111*
9. THE ACURA   *135*
10. LOVE SONGS   *147*
11. HELLHOUND   *161*
12. WINDMILLS   *177*

SPRING

13. LORD OF THE FLIES   *195*
14. CEREBRAL PASTRY   *209*
15. END OF THE INNOCENCE   *223*
16. HUCK   *237*

AFTERWORD   *241*
ACKNOWLEDGMENTS   *247*
RESOURCES   *251*

Author's Note

All names, places, and events are factual.

Introduction

We read often of youngsters who grow up with violence and despair, but there remains another coming of age, one experienced by adolescents in cities, suburbs, and small towns. This is the story of Dave Bettencourt and Beth Sunn, who came from one of those places.

Dave was irreverent, quick, restless, and kind. He had three goals as his senior year began. He wanted to get into a good college—though not to study what his parents believed he should. He wanted to start on the varsity basketball team, as much in memory of his dead grandfather as for himself. He planned an aggressive campaign for class clown, and he was betting that his humor, which owed much to Monty Python and *Saturday Night Live,* would get him the votes.

He did not plan on publishing an underground newspaper, or zine, with his friends—that just happened. Before the first issue, he did not foresee big trouble—but it came, and kept coming, from teachers, his principal, and the in crowd. He did not plan on falling for Beth Sunn—but that happened, too.

Beth never imagined where things would lead the night she met Dave at his brother's pool party. Beth was sentimental, flippant, and smart, but, like Dave, was bored by much of school. She was a cheerleader, newly into rap, and her fashion and speech borrowed heavily from African-American culture, which she knew from movies and TV. At thirteen, she'd been arrested for taking her father's car for a joyride. She was almost fifteen now. The Bettencourts didn't know quite what to make of her. Neither, at times, did her parents.

They lived in New England, in a place, on the American scene, midway between David Lynch and Norman Rockwell. Dave's town wasn't big enough to have a fast-food restaurant or a mall, but each was less than twenty minutes away, and Boston and Providence were within commuting distance. A small town, in the most densely populated corridor of the nation.

Their time was unlike any before. Sex suffused the culture, and desire for material things was a national passion. Microchips had transformed leisure and work. Drugs and alcohol were temptations beginning in grammar school. Violence did not affect Beth and Dave to the extent it did some of their urban peers, but it was never far away.

Mostly, this is a story of ageless firsts. It's about falling in love, and keeping secrets, and telling lies. It's about thinking deeply and not thinking at all, about taking risks and paying consequences, about fitting in and standing out—about what it means to grow up.

FALL

▲ *Gene Cazeault and Dave Bettencourt, distributing the first edition of* Total Godhead.

Chapter 1

TOTAL GODHEAD

"Welcome to the first edition of Total Godhead. *We at
T. G. Headquarters open our arms and hearts to all of
you who wish to read our wonderful paper."*

—TERRY GIMPELL

Dave Bettencourt was pale when he came into the senior quad
that September afternoon. He spoke solemnly, which was not
like him at all.

"Chief knows it's us," he told Brian Ross. "Chief" was Steve
Mitchell, their principal.

"How'd he find out?" Brian said.

"He called the cops."

"You're kidding."

"Nope."

"Jesus."

Burrillville High had never seen an underground newspaper before. In the two days since theirs had materialized in
lockers throughout the school, Dave and his staff had kept to
the shadows. No one could figure out who was behind this
publication with the bizarre name *Total Godhead.* Maybe it

was Satanists, as one girl speculated. Maybe it was a teacher who'd gone over the edge. Maybe troublemakers from out of town or, more likely, some loser kid on drugs.

Even a careful reading didn't provide an answer. Each of *Total Godhead*'s thirteen articles was bylined—with names like Toilet Duck, A. Nonymous, and Sum Yung Gi. The only clue that looked legitimate was a local post office box, through which *Godhead* hoped to solicit fan mail, subscription orders, and gifts. Among the suggested gifts were Elvis stamps and condoms, "unused, of course."

"What did the cops do?" Brian asked Dave.

"Went to the post office. They traced it to my dad."

"They can do that?"

"They did it."

"Now what?"

"I don't know."

There was funny stuff in *Godhead*—you'd have to be a dweeb not to get it. Like the the story about meatball stomping, or the one about the human bludgeoned by baby seals. But some of *Godhead* was irredeemably tasteless. One article was an ode to obscenity—a gratuitous listing of such items as rectal thermometers, nasal fluids, roadkill, and hairy gnome scrotums, whatever they were. One article was inspired by "Cop Killer," the controversial song by black gangsta rapper Ice-T. One reprinted the lyrics from "Rape Me," a song by Nirvana, Kurt Cobain's band.

Another piece slammed classmates—by name and with exacting physical descriptions, lest there be doubt of who was being savaged. "I'm sick of the way you dress" is how one boy was ridiculed. "What the heck is it with the little beard thing?" went the attack on another kid. The sharpest words were directed at the class president, Justin Michaelman, who'd been elected in a stunning upset over Matt Stone, a clean-cut, three-letter athlete who'd held the office junior year. "How the heck did he become president?" *Godhead* said of Michaelman. "What a moron."

Dave and Brian withdrew to a corner of the quad, where they might have privacy while figuring out what to do next. The quad was nothing like what its Ivy League–sounding name suggested—only a rectangle of lawn with scraggly shrubs, a single tree, and a manhole cover that boys (never girls) periodically and with great ceremony pried off, as if something rare and wonderful lurked in the darkness below. The quad's sole furnishings were a trash barrel, a rusted barbecue grill, and two picnic benches decorated with obscenities and declarations of undying love. But permission to hang out there was a senior privilege, and even on inclement days seniors flocked to it, if only to flaunt their status to underclassmen.

Another senior privilege was hosting this Friday's get-acquainted dance, an annual hazing. Since lunch, the mood in the quad had been giddy as seniors made their plans. Could they get away with hosing down the freshmen? Coating them with Crisco oil, catsup, or WD-40? Freshmen were clueless— you could make them kiss your naked butt if you wanted to. The challenge was determining the precise location of the line that Chief and his assistant principal wouldn't let you cross.

Dave and Brian's privacy didn't last. It was just too obvious: Something was going down, something with a better buzz than a dance.

"What's going on?" said Joel Waterman, Dave's best friend.

"We got caught."

"You're shitting me."

"Uh-uh," Dave said. "Chief called the cops."

"What do we do now?"

"I don't know. Maybe just forget about it."

"We can't do that."

"Did he say what he was going to do?" Joel said.

"No."

That wasn't a good sign.

"I think we have to talk to him," said Jason Ferguson.

And Ferg was right: If *Godhead* was to go forward, they really had no choice. Off they went: seven boys led by Dave out of the quad and into the administrative wing of Burrillville High, home of the Broncos, a public school with 825 kids in a town of almost seventeen thousand.

Chief did not look amused when the boys got to his office. He looked bigger than he was—and he already was very big, a six-three, broad-shouldered, dark-haired man who sometimes wore a full feathered headdress when teaching students about his people, the Penobscot Indians of Maine.

"We're the staff of *Total Godhead*," Dave said.

"Come in," Chief said.

He closed the door.

The coffee was always fresh in the principal's office, the jellybean jar always full. Chief had decorated with pictures: of his wife, his stepdaughter, his faculty, a black-and-white shot of his grandfather in ceremonial garb greeting John F. Kennedy when he visited Maine as a presidential candidate in 1960. The biggest display, most of a wall, was of kids—this one a state policeman now, that one a Hollywood actor, this other one still in college. There were pictures of this year's juniors and seniors, of cheerleaders and athletes, of kids in prom finest. You had to search to find one without a smile.

But Chief's office had multiple personalities, and now, as he went eye to eye with each of the boys, it seemed stuffy and small, a place they gladly would have escaped.

They weren't members of the in crowd, these boys, weren't losers or jocks—didn't fit neatly into a clique, which Chief suspected was a point of pride. Joel Waterman, a slender boy with a sharp tongue who was the school's most computer-literate student. Brian Ross, who owned seven guitars, knew more than three hundred rock 'n' roll songs, and bore a passing resemblance to Kramer on *Seinfeld*. Ferg, a contemplative kid who wore an earring, shaved the bottom half of his head, and had a bent for industrial design. Jason Cote, an artist and a lover of science fiction whose red 1989 Pontiac Firebird was the most coveted car at Burrillville High. Bruce Walls, who had a future in engineering but currently was into cigarettes and girls. Michaelman, an actor and artist who was never satisfied with any way he wore his hair.

And David Paul Bettencourt, who wrote for *Godhead* as Terry Gimpell, a pseudonym he'd plucked from the air.

Dave was skinny and tall, a boy with short dark hair, brown eyes, and the first traces of a mustache and beard. His attire was characteristic of his generation: baggy pants, T-shirt, Reeboks, cap worn backward. (Before entering the principal's office, he'd put it in his pocket.) Chief knew Dave was an honors student, that his family was neither rich nor poor, that both parents lived at home, and that he was not an only child. He knew Dave was not known to need any rehabilitation or counseling—not a head case. He knew Dave was seventeen and wanted to go to college. He knew . . . well, Chief didn't really know much more than that. Half the kids at Burrillville High were like Dave, moving through the mainstream with barely a splash.

Except now that he reflected, Chief realized how superficial his perception had been. He remembered the junior prom, when Dave, walking arm-in-arm with another boy—a boy!— had smiled and blown kisses to the crowd during the Grand

March, still hallowed after all these years. He remembered last spring's underclassmen awards night when Dave, to the mortification of many, especially his old English teacher, a staid sort, had done jumping jacks across the stage. He remembered the final day of school, when Dave had conspired with some of these same boys to create a fake murder scene—stage blood, body outline, police tape and all, very realistic—in one of the busiest corridors of the school.

And maybe that was just the warm-up. Not three weeks ago, Chief had gone into the cafeteria and found Dave presiding over a picnic. He and the gang had spread a blanket on the floor, sat down, and started on their sandwiches. It was the second day of school.

"You're so queer," a girl at a nearby table said.

"Like you make a difference in my life, space ghost woman," Dave replied, to a dirty look. "Look—it rained. What can I do? I don't control the weather."

Chief had decided to let it pass, even though he could have nailed the picnickers on a technicality—surely there was some rule somewhere about proper conduct at lunch. "This is unique," is all he said. "Just don't block the door."

Chief held the silence for one moment more.

That's interesting, he thought. Michaelman, Ferguson, Cote, Walls, and Ross—they were the ones who'd been slammed in *Godhead*. So it had been a dupe. They'd slammed themselves.

Chief explained to the boys why he'd taken the extraordinary measure of going to the police after he'd been unable to determine, through the regular channels, who was behind *Godhead*. "The thing I really take umbrage with is when you do a tune on an individual," he said. "Everyone is a human being. Everyone is a valuable person. I don't want anyone to be abused by anyone else. I want people to be tolerant of other lifestyles."

Chief understood tolerance in a way these kids, all middle-class suburban white boys, did not. Son of a Passamaquoddy woman and a Penobscot man, Mitchell had come of age in an era when white punks went to school dances specifically for the chance to jump redskins. He knew what it was like to be assigned to the lowest track in school because of the color of his skin. Growing up one of fourteen children in a three-bedroom house on a reservation, he knew what it took to get along in life. At a minimum, it took respect.

His background and profession had also given Chief antipathy for violence. He'd been concerned when he'd read "Assassin's Corner," a *Godhead* column that opened with the declaration: "I don't want to kill everyone. Just the people I don't like. That's the attitude one must take in order to become a true cold-blooded killer." Was it a put-on? Probably. But these were not the days to take chances. Just last year, bad blood between the hockey team and a group of kids who called themselves MSP, Minority Street Posse, had nearly escalated to a brawl. Rumors of guns, knives, and gang warfare had swept Burrillville High. One of MSP's founders, Jeff Fague, Dave's basketball teammate, had wound up in court after bloodying a kid in a fistfight at school. And while everything had fizzled after Chief intervened, the trouble with MSP had been a reminder that this wasn't just a small town in northwest Rhode Island. This was America at the close of the twentieth century.

"First we had the posse. Now we've got the assassins," Chief said. "I thought it was time I got out my war club!"

The boys laughed. Chief was cool! This was turning out OK, after all.

Taste also was an issue with Mitchell, and he told the *God-head*ers some of their material had gone too far. The lyrics from "Rape Me," for example. All those descriptions of the male reproductive organ.

"I said: 'Is this some male bonding, some male ritual?' "

More laughter.

Overall, Chief applauded the energy and imagination behind *Godhead.* "It's absolutely creative," he said. "I'd like to tap that creativity into something very positive."

Fair enough. But would he blow their cover? Part of the fun of *Godhead* was writing any damn thing you pleased, but part was the skullduggery. Playing mind games with the whole school was awesome.

"We'll keep it on the QT," Chief said. He was going out on a limb. He knew he was obligated to mention *Total Godhead* to his superintendent, who would inform the school committee, which answered to a taxpaying populace that was not unanimous in its vision of what public education should be. His superiors would not like his decision, Chief knew. Condoms and hairy gnome scrotums did not win battles in the public-relations war.

"Thanks, Chief," Dave said.

"Yeah, thanks," the others said.

Mitchell had only three requests: no school equipment was to be used for *Godhead*; future issues of the zine were to be submitted to him before distribution; and nothing was to be in bad taste.

And if Mitchell really believed that's how it would go down, he was kidding himself.

▲ *Mary Lee Drouin.*

Chapter 2

DROUIN

*"Education's job today is less in purveying information
than in helping people to use it—that is, to exercise their
minds."*

—THEODORE R. SIZER, PROFESSOR OF EDUCATION, BROWN UNIVERSITY

"Has anyone told you this is the best year of your life?" Mary
Lee Drouin said to her twenty-seven honors English students.
It was September 3, the first day of class.

"It's not," Drouin went on. "This year is hell! It's a hard
year but it's filled with wonderful, wonderful things. Try and
enjoy it. Don't expect too much from it, but expect a lot of
yourself as you proceed through it."

So this was Drouin, a teacher so beloved by her students
that many wrote her poems and gave her gifts, often years after
they'd moved on in the world. Dave had never had Drouin,
but he knew her by reputation. He'd heard she was demanding but good, very good, maybe the best at Burrillville High.
He'd heard she was funny, honest, and fair, and that she had
no use for "chalk and talk," a teaching method based on re-
gurgitation of facts—a guaranteed ticket to Snooze City. He

knew she had another life, as songwriter and lead singer for Pendragon, a New England folk band that had released several albums and was in demand for concerts. When coaxed, or as a reward for exemplary behavior, she would sing her students ballads.

Even when not singing, her voice was extraordinary—first soothing, then cajoling, now carried away with the power of the passage she was reading or erupting into great contagious laughter that carried into the hall. Storms of emotion sometimes swept Drouin up and she was not ashamed to cry; but usually, there was joy in her face. She was thirty-eight, a shade taller than average, a woman with brown hair and eyes of blue—the blue of a tropical lagoon, when the light was right. Her house, which she shared with her husband and daughter, who was Dave's age, was three centuries old. It was near the Blackstone River, which flows south from Worcester, Massachusetts, to Pawtucket, Rhode Island, birthplace of the American Industrial Revolution, inspiration for many of Pendragon's songs. Drouin's ancestors had crossed the Atlantic to work in the mills.

She taught in a room constructed like any at Burrillville High, a building showing the wear and tear of twenty-five years of scrimping on maintenance. The walls were cinderblock. The windows had lost their seals. The leaking roof had finally been fixed, but when it rained, the runoff sounded like a toilet flushing as it drained through plastic pipe that hung beneath the ceiling. The PA system was scratchy and loud and, it seemed, invariably interrupted at the worst moments. Her computer was an antique Apple, and it often ate files, just as her printer often skipped lines, forgot letters, and perpetrated other atrocities upon the printed word. But this was merely a cost of doing business in the public classroom, a place Drouin still loved after a decade and a half of teaching.

Her decor mimicked her feelings. That spiritless concrete—she'd exorcised it with plants, posters, and student artwork she'd collected over the years. Like Chief, Drouin delighted in photographs of kids and they were everywhere: her desk, the walls, the shelf beneath the windows. She had a nineteenth-century school bell, used to begin meetings of her Dead Poets Society, a literary discussion group inspired by the movie; its motto, like the movie's, was *carpe diem:* "seize the day." Her desk was a mess of papers, pencils, and books, among them an autographed copy of Ted Sizer's *Horace's Compromise,* which calls for a radical restructuring of American high school education. Drouin drank coffee in class. She kept a tea cart in one corner of her room, and students at midmorning could help themselves to hot chocolate or tea, or the doughnuts or cookies someone always brought in. Traditionalists on the faculty didn't see what eating had to do with learning, and some were certain a hippie lurked in her past, but they were wrong. Drouin simply had the touch.

"These are the things that impress me," she said that first day. She ticked off a list, which Dave and his classmates wrote down.

Creativity was first, followed by imagination. "Don't be afraid to use it," Drouin said. "It's a place where we're safe. How can anyone tell you your imagination is wrong?" Risk-taking was on her list, along with kindness, gracious acceptance of criticism, and integrity, which students correctly took to mean no cheating or plagiarism. "There are so many other things I can fix," she said, "but I can't fix those who have no integrity." Drouin also valued competition, but only of one kind. "The only person I want you to compete with is yourself," she said. "In my eyes, each and every one of you is important and cannot be measured against the other." She most admired people who had what she called a life of the mind.

Without ever having spoken to him, Drouin knew Dave was that kind of kid. She'd read his summer assignment: three short stories he'd delivered in a colorfully decorated binder—untypical, for a boy. One story was a long, elaborate fantasy with the flavor of Tolkien. Another was set in south-central Los Angeles, scene of rioting in the wake of the 1992 Rodney King verdict; with graphic detail and dialogue, Dave attempted to capture the flavor of inner-city street life ("Yo, whassup with you, nigga! What you trippin' or somethin?" "Yo, das cool!" "Yo . . . drive-by!"). Dave's third story was "A South Central L.A. Success Story," about Dave Warner, an African-American teenager who is raised by his father after his mother is killed in a holdup. In his very first varsity basketball game, Dave helps his team to victory and, afterward, talks his good friend Jay out of using a 9-mm semiautomatic pistol to settle a dispute.

He's a good writer, Drouin thought. Only seventeen, of course, with the roughness you'd expect at that age, but already very descriptive—a painter with words.

The boys were at the back of the room at Burrillville High that day in August when *Godhead* was conceived. They'd come for a meeting that Mindy Ryan, yearbook faculty adviser, had called to brainstorm themes for the 1993 *Review,* permanent record of the most important year yet in the lives of 175 teenagers.

Ryan was an English teacher, a highly organized and conscientious woman whose yearbook duties required her to serve two masters: kids and the administration. She was middle-aged, single, a conservative dresser, respected by her colleagues for her competence and commitment to her work.

Dave didn't like her ideas for the yearbook.

Ryan didn't like his. She was beginning to wonder if she'd erred in naming him sports editor.

Ryan was friends with Dave's mother, Leslie Bettencourt, a biology teacher in another town. She'd taught Dave sophomore year and was sufficiently impressed with his scholarship to give him an 88 for a final grade. She knew Dave, or thought she did. Dave won science fairs, competed in statewide history fairs, and played junior-varsity basketball. His clothes were the best. He always said his "please"s and "thank-you"s, and he was generous and kind. And quiet. Until last spring, that was the image she had of Dave: a good kid . . . *quiet but good.* So what was the deal with the jumping jacks at underclassmen awards night? What was all this talk lately about Dave planning to campaign—campaign!—for class clown? What was this nonsense now in the back of the room as the boys suggested class superlatives?

"Most Likely to Serve a Lengthy Jail Sentence," Dave joked.

"Most Likely to Recede," a friend said.

Please, Ryan said.

"We should just make our own yearbook," said Joel, yearbook co-editor.

"Yeah!" said Dave. "I have all the stuff to do it on the computer at my house."

Someone suggested a takeoff of a Nirvana album cover. It would show a picture of a classmate whose most distinctive feature was body odor; instead of "Smells Like Teen Spirit," title of Nirvana's biggest hit, they would plug in the name of the offending boy. The boys in the back of the room were silly over that.

But the production considerations of a book were intimidating. And who had that kind of cash?

"Why not an underground newspaper?" said Brian Ross. Brian even had the name: *Total Godhead,* the title, minus the expletive "fucking," of an obscure Nirvana single. Brian had come across it while browsing on Providence's East Side, the coolest place to hang out in Rhode Island.

"All right!" said Dave.

A week into the school year, Ryan had another yearbook meeting, this time at night. Dave and Joel slipped away before it was over. Prowling the darkened corridors of Burrillville High, they taped flyers to ceilings and walls. "The *Blueprint* may bring you the good news of B.H.S., but what about the real news? *Total Godhead.* Coming Soon."

The only person Dave and Joel ran into was a janitor buffing floors.

"We're just putting up something for the *Blueprint*," Dave said. The *Blueprint* was Burrillville High's official student newspaper.

"Fine, go ahead," the janitor said. "But you shouldn't be in here this late."

The buzz was everywhere the morning of September 18 when students opened their lockers and found a four-page, unevenly photocopied publication with a weird name in large Gothic type.

Total Godhead went to homerooms and then along to class. It wound up in the cafeteria, the library, bathrooms, teachers' lounges, the gym. One teacher taped it to his bulletin board with a sign: "I support free journalism." Another teacher didn't understand the need for secrecy, wasn't pleased that, as she saw it, the writers lacked the spine to use their real names. Some, like Drouin, were tickled. *Godhead* was predictably sophomoric, but it certainly didn't lack for creativity. It had humor—even to an adult.

"We feel this school needs some comic relief," Terry Gimpell wrote in the lead article. "Laugh with us. Hang it on your wall. But there is one simple demand we would like you to obey. Please do not try to figure out who we are. We want to be anonymous. We like to be anonymous. We will come out of the shadows when the time comes, but until then, just chill."

But whether you could chill depended on who you were.

Rapper punks thought *Godhead* was cool, so they chilled. So did the losers, kids denied front stage because of appearance, unrefined social skills, or some inner need to go it alone. Losers saw *Godhead* as a voice for them, the disenfranchised, and automatically assumed one of their own must have put it out. Some honors seniors found *Godhead* refreshingly different, if crude in spots. Kids who weren't anchored in any group—free spirits like the *Godhead*ers—appreciated the zine. "Never sell out, and *never ever* lose your balls," one such girl said in a letter that arrived in Dave's dad's post office box a few days after publication. The *Blueprint* named an investigative team to ferret out who was behind *Godhead*. As the *Godhead*ers observed these developments, they could barely contain themselves. When no one was looking, Dave and Joel exchanged high fives.

The strongest reaction came from the in crowd, which had been slammed in an article titled "A Letter to the Plastics." It was written by Theodore Grocki III, pseudonym of Rob Eddy, the class of '93's top male scholar:

> My commentary is about the occupation of three quarters of the school. EVERYONE IS PLASTIC! Why can't people start their own trends? Wear a McGregor shirt instead of a Champion shirt. Start a different fad. Are people so idiotic that they have to conform to what their friends wear, say or do? You people always talk the same old "in" crowd

stuff all day long. IT BITES! Face reality! Stick your balls in
a situation. Go out on a limb.

There was no question that the in crowd ruled at Burrillville
High. They'd occupied the top of the social pyramid since
fourth grade, when cliques began to coalesce in the future class
of '93.

From the outside, the in crowd was monolithic—impene-
trable and unfriendly, viewed from where the losers were. In-
crowd kids played sports or were cheerleaders. They had cars.
They dressed alike, an understated preppie look this year with
an accent on Champion clothing, a line of athletic wear that
had an expedient echo in their theme song: Queen's "We Are
the Champions." They liked to drink and they threw the best
parties. None was handicapped or ugly. For the most part,
they dated their own, sat together at lunch, and clustered in
the corridors between classes. At dances, they owned the middle of the floor.

Seen from the inside, the in crowd was diverse. You did not
have to be well-to-do, although some were. Children of divorced parents and those from intact families were repre-
sented. Kids headed to college belonged, as did kids who'd be
pumping gas for a living. Some were indeed insufferable snobs,
but many were down-to-earth. Their common bond was
knowing they were the in crowd—and that everyone else,
roughly 90 percent of their class, was not.

The in crowd was not humorless, and many thought *Godhead* was funny. Others dismissed it as yet another bizarre em-
anation from the minds of those pesty weird kids. Beth Stone,
an athlete and former class officer, was pissed.

"They don't even know the people they're talking about,"
Beth said as she read *Godhead* before World Literature, another course Drouin taught. "There are a lot of people I think

are fake. And then I get to know them and there's a whole other person inside. Rrrrr! I'm sitting here getting so mad I can't read it anymore!"

She wasn't the only one angry, as Dave would soon discover.

Once, Dave had wanted to be an astronaut. After watching *Top Gun,* the coolest thing to be was a fighter pilot, and by early high school, he'd decided he wanted an appointment to the Air Force Academy. This pleased his parents, especially his mom, who won national awards for her innovative science programs. Who knew? Maybe someday he'd be on the space shuttle, on which Leslie herself had considered flying before Christa McAuliffe was launched to a fiery death.

By the end of junior year, when he was arranging his senior curriculum, Dave's interest in science, and fighter planes, was flagging. He signed up for physics and precalculus only to avoid a hassle at home. He had no desire to take Spanish 3, but he did because colleges for some reason liked foreign languages on transcripts, and because Leslie had fought to add Spanish to a curriculum that had offered only Latin and French. He took health and gym because the school made him—but that was OK, you could shoot hoops in gym and health was taught by John Wignot, varsity basketball coach. That left two electives. He picked Drouin's English and journalism/creative writing, taught by Dick Martin, whom he'd had for English junior year. At seventeen, Dave envisioned a career in stand-up comedy or sports broadcasting. He figured writing would serve him well in either.

The early days in physics and Spanish were educational disasters.

Before class the third day of school, Dave went to the board and wrote: "Sex is not the answer. Sex is the question. Yes is the answer."

"David, get that off there," the teacher said. She was a pleasant woman in her thirties, always sharply dressed and fastidious with her makeup and hair. In high school, she had been Miss Rhode Island National Teenager, an accomplishment she sometimes still mentioned to people she met.

"I learned it in sex ed," Dave said.

"This is Spanish."

"I learned it in Spanish sex ed."

"Awesome!" Joel commented. It was volatile, Joel and Dave together in a class neither cared for.

Moments later, the teacher was conjugating the verb *comer*, Spanish for "to eat."

When Dave heard "comen," he said, "Conan the Barbarian! Conan's brother!"

"David."

"This whole language is weird!"

Physics was no better. It was taught by Ed Wilk, a white-haired, highly intelligent man who spiced up lectures by writing words right to left or bumping into furniture. Rumor had it Wilk had built a boat in his basement—realizing too late that it was too big to get out the door. (The rumor wasn't true, but Wilk was amused when it resurfaced every September.) Wilk had been at Burrillville High thirty years, long enough to know that trying to get anywhere with seniors who didn't care was wasted energy. If students had genuine interest, fine, he would put out for them; the best he hoped for the rest was some semblance of order. Dave passed his time in physics playing on a computer, roughing out *Godhead* articles, and writing letters to his girlfriend, Beth Sunn, a sophomore at North Smithfield High School, in the next town over. They'd been going steady since July, and already Beth, fourteen, was certain she'd be spending the rest of her life with Dave.

Early on, Dave tried stunts with Drouin, including once when he and Joel brought walkie-talkies to class and kept up a running dialogue with them, but Drouin quickly put an end to such nonsense. That was cool. All that stuff the first day about imagination, creativity, a life of the mind—Dave had discovered it wasn't your ordinary beginning-of-the-year bullshit. Drouin delivered. As he sat there every morning, watching as she drank her hazelnut coffee, leaned across her podium and filled them with her love of words, Dave began to wish he'd stood up to his mom and taken Drouin's World Lit instead of physics or precalculus.

For her part, Drouin saw Dave as a work in progress. He had a past, but she knew it was not where he dwelled; he had a future, but except for applying to college, she knew it was something he'd worry about later. Dave moved in the present, with great speed and sudden shifts in direction. In class, it was Dave who took first stab at questions, even when he wasn't sure he had the right answer; Dave who always volunteered to read his essays; Dave who motivated his peers when Drouin broke the class into smaller groups; Dave who picked up the occasional flat spot with a joke. Sometimes he played too obviously to the crowd, but that, Drouin knew, was Dave.

"The big issue for him will be learning to control all these incredible capacities," Drouin said. "A lot of this year will be like going up to a stove and realizing, '*Ssss!* That's hot! I have to figure out whether or not I want to risk touching it again.' Sometimes, he will."

And sometimes, she thought, it would be best to let him.

▲ *Leslie Bettencourt and her firstborn.*

Chapter 3

STARS

"Son to Mr. and Mrs. Paul L. Bettencourt of 178 Round Top Road, Harrisville, Feb. 14."

—Providence *Evening Bulletin*, February 24, 1975

Leslie Ferry met Paul Bettencourt, the man she would marry, in the summer of 1968. She was nineteen, a sophomore at Rhode Island College, whose purpose was making teachers. Paul walked into her life, quite literally. She was living at home in Johnston, a suburb of Providence, and there he was one summer evening—this dark, thin man of twenty-one, in her living room, at her father's invitation. Don Ferry was a grocer by day, a comedian and singer by night, and Paul wanted to hire him for a Hawaiian night his mother was putting on for her Catholic church.

When her parents had gone to bed, Leslie sat with Paul. He was different from the boy she'd just broken up with: more mature, funnier, not intimidated by her academic success and passion for biology. They talked past midnight, and a few days later Leslie appeared at the Hawaiian night, ostensibly to watch her dad perform. Paul took her out when it was over, and soon he was sending her carnations and cards he made himself. "My mother said she'd worry if I went to your apartment," one read, "let's go to mine and let your mother worry!" Read another: "I'll give you a big box of chocolates if you let me nibble!" They went steady that fall, a courtship of bowling, movies, and family gatherings at the Ferrys'. Paul gave Leslie a friendship ring for Christmas and an engagement ring on Valentine's Day, 1969. On July 4, 1970, a month after Leslie graduated from college, they were married.

After a honeymoon in Florida, Leslie began teaching at the first place she'd been offered a job: the public high school in Lincoln, Rhode Island, two towns east of Burrillville. Paul left his job with a defense contractor for radio sales, a move that led to a marketing business he later ran from home. As they moved through their twenties, the Bettencourts had new desires. They wanted their own home, in a place where trees were plentiful, taxes modest, and the people more or less like them. They wanted to start a family.

Nipmuc Indians were first in Burrillville. They hunted, fished, gathered nuts, and planted corn, and when settlers began arriving from Providence in the late 1600s, they quietly slipped away, leaving nothing but stone foundations and the name of a future village: Pascoag, a Nipmuc subtribe. The English wanted land. It was not forgiving land, none in New England was, but when trees were felled, rocks cleared, and stone walls built, it could support farms. Smiths and Arnolds raised livestock and grew potatoes and beans, crops not fussy about soil. Cider was pressed and beer brewed, and some of a family's meager surplus could be bartered for spices or calico, hints of a better life none would have.

If not for water, Burrillville would have slumbered through the nineteenth century. But the Blackstone Valley has water in abundance—rivers and streams that could be easily dammed, that could turn wheels to power machines that would entice entrepreneurs and provide a growing class of workers a steady wage. The first mills were simple: a wheel, a few gears and belts, and a shack to keep the weather away. Grist and lumber were the first products, but as the nineteenth century opened, cotton and wool had become more profitable. By century's end, as steam replaced water and small mills grew into sprawling factories, Burrillville, named for James Burrill, Jr., a U.S. senator, was a mighty economic engine. The town's population nearly doubled from 1850 to 1900, surpassing six thousand. The Irish came first; then the French Canadians, who by the turn of the century had become the largest group of non-English people in town. Libraries, hotels, saloons, churches, schools, and two newspapers were opened. Three railroads came into town and an electric railway connected Burrillville to larger population centers east, providing easy access to Spring Lake and Pascoag Reservoir, whose waters were pure. Where Nipmucs once fished, summer colonies were built by an emerging middle class.

The height of prosperity was between the World Wars, an era associated with Austin T. Levy, who left New York City in 1909 to seek his fortune. Levy succeeded as none before him in Burrillville had. His mill, the Stillwater Company, established in 1912, gave him his fortune, and with it he built mill housing for his workers and, for himself, the finest residence in town. He and his wife, June Rockwell Levy, a *Mayflower* descendant, kept a plantation in the Bahamas. They served on community boards, were active in Republican politics, and became the biggest benefactors the town would ever see. Before they died, the Levys had given Burrillville two schools, two post offices, a community theater, a courthouse, a library, a bridge, the town hall, and, next to the high school, a hockey rink, home of the Burrillville Broncos.

By 1975, when Leslie and Paul moved into town, the boom was essentially over. The textile industry had abandoned Burrillville for the South and overseas, and those mills that hadn't been torn down or claimed by arson were empty or had a new use, in plastics or electronics, products with value in a new age. By the nineties, Burrillville's past survived largely in names. Some hearkened to the Nipmucs—Wolf Hill, Badger Mountain—while others were echoes of ancient economies—Steere Farm Road, Railroad Avenue. Still others were names of the town's villages: Harrisville, where Burrillville High was; Wallum Lake, site of a chronic-disease hospital, originally a sanitorium and now the town's largest employer; Pascoag, where the vaudeville hall was used for storage.

But Burrillville was not dead; once again, land had given it life. There was fifty-six square miles of land in town, no more suited than before for agriculture, but acceptable for any number of raised ranches. New immigrants came from the cities and from out of state, exclusively whites at first, with small numbers of African-Americans, Hispanics, and other ethnic groups as time went on. They came for open space at affordable prices, and because the good jobs in a changing economy were only a commute away. Burrillville was on the western slope of a triangle connecting Boston, Providence, and Worcester—a region whose future was tied to the information and service industries. Burrillville's population grew more than 60 percent in the 1970s and 1980s. Unlike their predecessors, these newcomers brought their income with them—from law offices, doctors' practices, universities, computer and software firms. There were still families living in trailers and glorified tar-paper shacks in Burrillville, but the median household income was higher than the national. Many middle-class needs could be met in town. Burrillville had a half-dozen video stores, four pizza joints, three package stores, fifteen bars and restaurants with liquor licenses, a bank with an ATM machine, a gun shop, a tanning salon, and four Catholic churches, three Baptist churches, and four of other Protestant denominations. People liked working with their hands, which kept a paint-and-wallpaper shop, a lawnmower-repair business, two hardware stores, and a lumberyard in business. What you couldn't get in town you didn't have to travel far to find. One mall was twenty minutes away and three more were within forty-five minutes.

It was a town still in transition.

Many of the older folks had been employed in the mills and could recall the day they'd shaken the hand of Levy, George P. Metcalf, or another of the owners who made millions off the backs of working men and women. They still got up at five-thirty each morning, as did their children and their children's children. Dinner was the meal at noon. Ham-and-bean suppers were the preferred fund-raiser for the village fire departments, which were all volunteer. In Pascoag, the fire siren still sounded at seven each evening . . . but when darkness settled, it was cable TV most everyone watched.

Future meeting past created strain, most visibly on such matters as recycling and development of Burrillville's remaining open space. But no issue rivaled spending, and no expense was greater than running the schools. Although the school committee set individual accounts, it could only propose a bottom line; the town council had final approval. Each spring, as predictably as the heralding of peep toads, the battle was renewed. Town councilmen considered themselves guardians of the tax rate, answerable to swamp Yankees who placed pothole repair high on their list of municipal priorities. The school committee, which had hired a progressive superintendent, took seriously its mandate of fashioning young minds. It did not believe education's highest calling was to teach youngsters to sign time cards in mills that no longer existed. But even on the school committee, things were rarely unanimous. As Steve Mitchell and his boss knew well, meetings of the school committee and the town council remained forums for citizens seeking notoriety the old-fashioned way, by stirring up the shit.

David Paul Bettencourt was born at Providence's Women & Infants Hospital on Valentine's Day, 1975. Wrapped in a blue blanket, he went home to a house Leslie and Paul had designed and built themselves. Set into a hill, the house was surrounded by evergreens, some of which would later be sacrificed for something more valuable than trees: an in-ground swimming pool.

Dave was an easy baby. He smiled, laughed, and traveled well, happy to be wherever his family was. At one, he was talking, having spoken his first word, *"abbondanza!"*—Italian for "abundance!"—after hearing it on a pizza commercial. Dave liked books, and his parents kept him in fresh supply, but he was passionate for TV: *Sesame Street; Sha Na Na,* which had the fifties songs he liked; *Star Trek,* which his parents watched fanatically; and any kind of sports program. Shortly after turning two, Dave was performing. At family get-togethers, he would entertain from his repertoire of songs. Dave was Don and Dolores Ferry's first grandchild, and for three years, until his brother, Dan, was born, he was the undisputed center of attention. Laura arrived three years after Dan.

The lessons the Bettencourts imparted to their children were ones their parents had taught them: Share. Pick up after yourself. Practice table manners. Don't fight with your siblings. Attend Mass on Sundays. Respect authority. Don't talk to strangers. Tell the truth. Choose your friends wisely. Treat others as you would have them treat you. And, fundamental to all: Embrace your family, for only they will always be there.

Before meeting Leslie, Paul had talked of moving to Phoenix, but there was none of that now . . . maybe when Laura was in college. As it was, the Bettencourts had to defend their move to Burrillville, which was fifteen miles from where they'd grown up—no inconsequential distance for Rhode Islanders, whose sense of scale is compressed by living in the smallest state. The defense was simple. Burrillville did not lack for playgrounds or ballfields. Three wilderness management areas and part of a state forest were in town. The ice-cream truck came around every summer, and the carnival rolled through town, and some ladies' auxiliary was always having a yard sale or a fair.

The first thing Dave wanted to be was a fireman. Next was a cowboy. By nursery school, he was into space. Mom took him to science museums and, with Paul, helped him build and launch model rockets. His favorite movie was *Star Wars;* his favorite toys, *Star Wars* figures. When he got a *Star Wars* pillowcase, he went to sleep with his head on Luke Skywalker, his hero, never on the side with the evil Darth Vader. To keep monsters away, he pulled the covers over his head. Sometimes he had nightmares about clowns, which terrified him for reasons he still cannot explain.

At night, coming home from somewhere in the car, Dave would lay back and look at the stars.

"Where are those, Mom?" he'd say. "Do they end? Have we ever gone there?"

As adolescence arrived, Dave was no goodie-goodie. How could he be? How could Joel, who lived a five-minute bike ride away? They were warriors! They threw snowballs at cars and launched bottle rockets at a neighbor's house, withdrawing like rural guerrillas to the safety of woods when the mission was done. They smashed pumpkins and sought treasure inside a house abandoned after an old lady died, although they dared not go in after dark. They built forts and lit fires with matches their parents didn't know they had. Dave went door-to-door collecting for a multiple sclerosis fund-raiser, then kept the money for himself. He developed a craving for driveway reflectors and signs. It was petty thievery, but it gave him a rush, and no one but his blood brother need ever know.

There were other developments, more significant in light of what lay ahead. Friends of Leslie and Paul had a son who introduced Dave to Dungeons and Dragons, the role-playing fantasy game that requires what Drouin valued: an imagination. He watched *Saturday Night Live,* and while he didn't get all of the humor, not initially, he got enough to know how cool people like Eddie Murphy and Martin Short were. In seventh grade, Dave's English teacher, Bill Eccleston, encouraged him to write whatever was in his head. What an awesome idea—writing what you want!

Influenced by the films of Lucas and Spielberg, Dave wrote fantasies. "The Adventures of Indiana Brousseau," one of his seventh-grade stories, married imagination with burlesque caricatures of himself and his friends. Set in the jungle, the story described a quest for a comic book. "If they found the hidden temple that it is in, got the comic book and got out," Dave wrote, "they would be on *Lifestyles of the Rich and Famous.*"

"Funny," Eccleston commented. "By all means continue."

On the evening of September 22, the day after the *Godhead* crew had visited Chief's office, Leslie parked her car and went into her house. Six teenage boys had taken over the downstairs family room. One was Dave. One was Joel. The rest were strangers.

"Hello," Leslie said.

"Hello, Mrs. B," they said.

There was a bit of chitchat and then Leslie went upstairs, into the main living quarters of their split-level house. She called for her son to come up.

"What is that in the family room?" she said.

"That's the *Godhead* crew," Dave said.

"Who *are* they?" Leslie said.

It was how they looked: their hair, long on some of them, partially shaved on others; one boy with a beard; the combat boots on one kid; the T-shirt with a heavy-metal slogan on another . . . and what was it with the earrings, anyway?

Dave told his mother that they were good kids, from good homes—just individuals, that's all.

"There are teachers in my school who would take one look at them and decide they're on drugs," Leslie said.

"They're not on drugs, Ma."

When Dave was younger, Leslie had had last say on his choice of friends. Gradually, she'd relinquished control— sooner than you could imagine, she knew, her boy would be on his own. But Leslie still carefully tracked the people in Dave's life. Over dinner, she would probe for details: What kind of grades does he get? Does he play sports? What do his parents do? Leslie knew Dave's old circle well; she and Paul had always welcomed friends at the house, where computers, video games, backboard, and swimming pool were big attractions. All right, Joel was here tonight. But where were Justin Dawes, Scott Bridge, Kevin Blanchette, and the rest of the old gang? Why hadn't she seen much of them lately?

It's starting out as quite some year, isn't it? Leslie thought. Dave had a new girlfriend, too, a kid who, in a different way, was as portentous as the *Godhead*ers.

Beth Sunn.

Would Leslie or Paul ever forget the first time they'd seen her? Those rings, the big hair, the lollipop condom on her fly? She'd turned up at a party Dan had hosted in July, and the way she talked—"Yo" this and "Dis" that, jive about "home-boys"—you'd think she was some street kid from Brooklyn, not the only daughter of two middle-class white professionals who lived in North Smithfield, Rhode Island. What time Dave wasn't spending with the *Godhead*ers, he was spending with Beth. The worst of it was, she was only fourteen. Four-teen! At fourteen, Leslie hadn't even been looking at boys. Why couldn't Dave still be dating Lauren Raspallo? Now *there* was a nice girl.

Dave went back downstairs. When Leslie joined them a short while later, they were spread out over the floor, dis-cussing *Godhead 2*. As psyched as they were leaving Chief's office, they were soon deflated. They'd been caught—after ex-actly two days! There had to be some way to even the score. Maybe they could put out two papers: a second issue of *God-head*, and another called *Total Scrodhead* or *Total Oddhead*. Maybe produce an issue in code, handing out decoders only to the lucky few. See what Chief had to say about that!

Leslie had seen the first *Godhead*, and, like the principal, she thought parts were in poor taste. But she was most concerned with libel, and she advised the boys to avoid it in *Godhead 2*.

"Do you have a student handbook?" she said.

"Yeah," Dave said.

"Did you check to see if there's anything in there on under-ground newspapers?"

"They've never had a paper, so they don't have to worry about it," Ferg said.

"No doubt there will be something in there next year," Cote predicted.

Ferg speculated that the biggest concern of the school com-mittee and superintendent Dennis Flynn would be the effect bad publicity might have on a proposed $6 million high school renovation and expansion project. Depending on Flynn's financing plan, it might have to be presented to voters.

" 'Those punks in the high school don't deserve six million dollars if they're coming up with underground newspapers!' " Dave said.

"Did your father see it?" Leslie said to Joel.

"Not yet." Donald Waterman was chairman of the school committee.

"It's gotten to Dr. Flynn," Brian said.

"Flynn is extremely straight-laced," Leslie said. "You have to understand what you're dealing with here." Leslie knew; she'd been on the search committee that had recommended hiring Flynn, in 1988. More recently, she'd dealt with him on the issue of adding Spanish to the curriculum.

"We should print, 'This is going to be the last issue due to outside influences,' " Joel said. "Then everybody's going to stop coming around."

"That's not a bad idea," Brian said.

Leslie said: "You could say, 'This is our last issue . . .' And then: 'Back by popular demand! Due to overwhelming response from our readers, *Godhead* resurrects!' " For the moment, Leslie was into it. It reminded her of something she'd missed in the sixties, when she'd been so intent on her degree.

Leslie went upstairs and the *Godhead*ers shifted to the corner of the family room where Paul had his office. Dave booted up his father's Macintosh computer and called up Pagemaker, a professional typesetting program Paul used for his business. Working from Michaelman's rough draft, Dave typed the lead story, a "Total Apology" to the kids they'd slammed. "Total Apology" didn't let on that the initial article had been a trick, or anything about Chief having found out. It was another scam.

"All right," Dave said. "What else?"

"How about a big centerfold of Mr. Mitchell?" Brian said. "Stick his head on, like, a naked lady."

"Oh, yeah, like we wouldn't be kicked out of school!" Dave laughed, then killed the idea.

Under his pseudonym, the Insipid Utopian, Joel had written an article taking a whack at kids who'd had a party behind a girl's house one night her parents were away. Most had gotten drunk, and the cops had chased everyone into the woods. Beth had gone to the party without Dave, which had almost led to a breakup on the eve of their two-month anniversary. Only after tears and angry words had they gone on.

"To all of you who want a good buzz," Joel had written, "play with a chainsaw." Dave typed the article onto the front page of *Godhead 2.* Like Joel, he didn't drink.

"Let's have our own superlatives," Michaelman said.

"Yeah, let's!" said Dave. See what Mindy Ryan, yearbook adviser, had to say about that.

"Awesome," Brian said. They could make it a write-in contest.

"OK," said Michaelman. "Most Likely to Die."

"How about Most Likely to Die in a Car Crash?" Brian said. But Dave didn't use it; in 1982, five Burrillville High boys leaving a party a week before graduation had died when their car crashed into a tree. A sixth boy, who'd received an appointment to West Point, remained in a coma in the hospital at Wallum Lake. Every year on the anniversary of the accident, an anonymous someone left fresh flowers at the crucifix and statue of the Virgin Mary that stood near the tree.

"You could just put Class Alcoholic," Brian said.

"Class Alcoholic: Male and Female," said Michaelman.

"That's going to be a close one," Brian said. He mentioned the names of two boys, both notorious drinkers.

"Least Likely to Get Laid," Michaelman said.

"Nuh, nuh, nuh," Dave said.

"Most Likely to Sprout Breasts?"

"Photocopies of your breasts!" Joel said.

He wanted to make it a contest, with prizes for anyone who could correctly identify the girls whose breasts were published. And why not? Breasts were everywhere—in movies, magazines, penciled on bathroom walls. Boys surveyed them, discussed them, imagined them lying in bed at night. Large breasts held a special fascination, and speculation about which girl in town had the absolute biggest was endless.

It was after nine when Paul came downstairs. He was not happy.

"How much longer are you going to be doing this?" he fumed. "I need to get on there."

"Not much longer," Dave said.

"How often are you going to be working on this thing?" Paul said. "It's taking up all your time. You haven't been doing your homework."

"I haven't had any." It was a lie.

"The mess last time was really bad."

"I cleaned it up."

"Yeah," Paul said, "two days later. I work here, you know. I don't appreciate a mess."

"OK. Right. Yup."

After a question about who was going to pay for printing *Godhead*—the boys said they were (but they weren't; they intended to sneak copies off any photocopying machine they could find)—Paul, still grumbling, went back upstairs.

"All right," Dave said. "Page two."

Dave had a story on racism at Burrillville High in mind for that one. He typed with confidence, the words spilling out at a remarkable clip.

▲ *Dave and friends, faking a fight at Burrillville High.*

Chapter 4

HAIRY GNOME SCROTUMS

*"If I had to do the same thing every day with like 300
billion other people—if I had to get up at eight o'clock
and then do piecework in some factory with 300,000
other people—I think I'd go insane."*

—DAVE BETTENCOURT

When students opened their lockers on their way to homeroom the morning of Tuesday, October 6, *Godhead 2* awaited.
A copy was on Drouin's desk and one had been slipped under
the door to Dick Martin's room. Another had been left in the
Blueprint office.

Like Martin, Drouin had pretty much concluded that Dave
was one of the people behind *Godhead.* She detected his
hand—and shameless motivation—in "A Standing O for Dr.
Flynn," an article by "head chef Terry Gimpell," as he now
called himself, that began by repeating two common complaints students had: Their school was cold in winter, and the
gymnasium sucked. "What about the good things that Dr.
Flynn and his staff are trying to do for us?" Gimpell wrote.
"Dr. Flynn, our superintendent of schools for all those illiter-

ates in our school, is trying to get a bond to renevate* our wonderful center o' learning. I don't hear any students praising him for trying to fix our school."

But that was the only piece in *Godhead 2* where diplomacy was attempted. Dave and company had shifted the line of decency, as Chief had urged—by approximately one degree. There was nothing as offensive as the "Rape Me" lyrics this time, but there were ample references to vomit, diarrhea, blood, various components of the male urinary tract, and that old chestnut, hairy gnome scrotums. There was a ballot for *Godhead* superlatives, including Most Likely to Stay Back, and Class Alcoholic.

If any theme could be said to dominate *Godhead 2,* temperance was it. The Insipid Utopian's message to those intoxicated partygoers ("play with a chainsaw") was there, along with a shot from the head chef himself: "Why do people go to school dances drunk like a skunk? Please, don't drink and dance."

The next morning, Dave was late for school. He rushed in. Accompanied by a couple of friends, another senior was waiting in the hall. Before Dave knew what was happening, the kid slammed him against the wall, pinning him there.

"Why are you writing stuff about me?" he demanded.

"I didn't write any stuff about you," Dave said, weakly.

But he had. "Remember when a certain junior refused to sit with a black kid at the junior prom last year?" Terry Gimpell had written on the second page of *Godhead 2.* "That is just one racist of our school. There are many more out there. We must deal with this situation. . . . To quote a friend of mine: 'Don't look at the color, look at the person.' That is exactly what must happen. 'Justice evolves only after injustice is defeated' was spoken by Malcolm X, and we must follow that."

*All words in quoted material are spelled as they originally appeared.

The kid knew Gimpell was fingering him. He'd heard Gimpell was Dave.

"I'm not a racist," he said. "I have lots of black friends in Providence." He denied refusing to sit at a table with Kelly O'Rourke and her date, an African-American from Connecticut.

"No one was named," Dave said, and now he was scared the kid was going to beat him up.

The kid was capable. He wasn't the toughest character at Burrillville High, but he could take care of himself. He hung with the in crowd. He drank. Later in the year, he would walk into a math class and coolly punch out some punk who'd been part of a gang that had jumped one of his hockey buddies in a darkened parking lot after a game.

And Dave—five-eleven, 125-pound Dave, the kid Paul Bettencourt sometimes joked looked like a starving Third Worlder, the way his T-shirts and trousers hung off him— Dave was no hood! He'd been in exactly two fights in his life: a fourth-grade shoving match during a game of kickball, and a fifth-grade fistfight with a neighbor who stole his baseball cards. ("I kicked his butt, I'm glad to say," Dave would later recall.) Dave could not get by on might. He needed humor, intelligence, and speed, but they weren't options now.

"You wrote it," the kid said.

"It's not true."

"I heard it was true."

"I didn't have anything to do with that paper. Honest!"

Dave was saved by John Wignot, who heard the commotion and stepped into the hall. Shaken but unhurt, Dave went to homeroom, where he told his story to Gene Cazeault, who wrote for *Godhead* as Toilet Duck.

Like Dave, Gene, seventeen, was into stunts. He liked passing out stickers of wrestler Andre the Giant, whom he and

Ferg had proclaimed *Total Godhead* mascot. He liked making people laugh, with humor that blended Chris Elliott and Kids in the Hall. Gene was bearded, weighed 220 pounds, had the thickest forearms of anyone at school, and was close to a black belt in karate. He could tell you the clip size of a TEC-9, favored weapon of Los Angeles street gangs, but he had no desire to get one of his own. He was the best artist to come through the school in years—art editor of the yearbook, a boy with the talent to be accepted into New York's prestigious Pratt Institute.

Gene knew what it meant to be bullied. He'd been a quiet kid in grammar school, but unlike Dave, he wasn't into scholastics or sports. He spent much of his time escaping kids who picked on him. Freshman year, Gene was blown away by a karate class at the Okinawan Temple in downtown Pascoag. This wasn't some matchbook school of martial arts—this was Shorin-Ryu, a style that emphasizes self-defense over gymnastics. Pain was not to be avoided in Shorin-Ryu; your knuckles, if you were serious, became callused like stone. Gene signed on, and he believed it was karate and art that had assured his survival at Burrillville High.

"That's cool. That's real cool," he said within earshot of the kid who'd roughed up Dave. The kid got the message.

Dave's incident was the hottest story moving across the school wires that day, all but forcing anyone who'd somehow missed out on *Godhead 2* to get a copy.

"Bunch of fags," some kids in Gene's English class said as they read the paper a few periods later.

"Oh, I'm a fag?" Gene said.

"You're in on it?"

"Yeah. I wrote that piece."

"Oh, we didn't mean it that way."

Gene was not the only one attempting, in his way, to mediate between Dave and those who'd felt *Godhead*'s scorn. Another was Matt Stone, whom Michaelman had upset for class president.

Matt was the class of '93's luminary, the kid who had the beautiful girlfriend, made high honors, and captained three sports, including hockey, supreme in Burrillville. Matt was handsome and tall, and adults who knew him believed someday he would be a leader of men. In fact, he wanted to be an army helicopter pilot. His girlfriend was Tami Menard, a freshman at Brown University and daughter of Barbara Menard, a high school math teacher, and hockey coach Mike Menard. Matt would be voted Most Likely to Succeed, and at graduation would receive the Outstanding Bronco Award, the highest honor the school could bestow. All of this might easily have gone to a boy's head in a town of seventeen thousand— but with Matt, none of it did. Son of a gravedigger and a town hall clerk, Matt was kind, a listener, sometimes a practical joker, and always a hard worker. Drouin, who had him in honors English, was sure there was a poet in him somewhere. It was the highest compliment she could give.

Matt was one of the few kids who'd correctly guessed that Dave and Joel were involved in *Godhead*. The irreverence, the wackiness, the caustic edge—Matt knew it had to be them. As the controversy over *Godhead 2* unfolded, Matt paid attention. This was as good as one of Drouin's ballads—who knew where it would end? He listened to the growing complaints that the *Godhead* crew didn't have the balls to use their real names. He listened to his good friend Gary Briggs, Jr., who didn't appreciate all this crap directed at drinkers. Unlike the kid who'd roughed up Dave, Gary wouldn't necessarily be discouraged by Gene or John Tebow, an even larger friend whom Dave was sticking close to these days. Rugged and tall, normally good-natured, Gary, bound for the marines, was one of the leaders of the in crowd. He had an idea of how to handle *Godhead*.

"We're getting too old to settle things with our fists," Matt said to Gary when they were alone. "Besides, there's freedom of the press. ["With freedom of the press comes responsibility," Matt said to Dave later.] See what happens with the next issue." Gary agreed to wait. But as Matt told Dave, there was no telling how long he would keep his cool.

Unlike the losers, whose existence was rarely acknowledged by the in crowd, Dave was on civil terms with many of them— even Gary Briggs, until now. But he knew he wasn't one of them, and never would be. His biggest complaint was that they always had secrets—and wanted you, an outsider, to never forget they did. Well, now Dave had a secret. . . .

With his father's laser printer, Dave printed hundreds of stickers. KISS ME I READ *T.G.,* one said. YO! *GODHEAD* RAPS! TERRY GIMPELL IS MY HERO. *TOTAL GODHEAD.* QUESTION AUTHORITY. By week's end, the stickers were on book covers, clothes, lockers, foreheads, toilet stalls, bus seats, and light switches. When Drouin called her Dead Poets Society to order that week, she saw a poster on the ceiling: MERRY HALLOWEEN FROM *TOTAL GODHEAD*! Even if you had no interest in the underground press, you had to have a sticker. That week, *Godhead* ruled.

Only one thing spoiled the fun: two letters to Mr. Gimpell that Dave received on Friday.

The letters were from someone choosing to be identified only as D. B. Lover—someone who claimed to be a girl at Burrillville High who knew Gimpell was Dave.

> I have had a secret desire for you since the end of our tenth grade. I know you have a girlfriend, a Miss Beth Sun. I was not happy when I found out that you were going out with a tenth grader especially from North Smithfield (land of the rich and snobbish). I *was* happy when I found out about the ending of the Lauren relationship. Your pretty, little nigger

of a rapper girlfriend will not stop me from getting you. It is
my obligation to my heart to end up with you in the final
chapter.

Hello?

I wonder what I could do to get rid of her. I promise I will
not hurt her physically in any way. I'm sick of hearing,
"Oh, did you see Dave Bettencourt's girlfriend. Yah, she is
pretty, hot, nice looking." When no one acknowledges me
or my friends looks. I mean, it is not like we are ugly or
nothing but please. You will probably be acquiring some
more of my letters in the future.
    Love 4-eva,
    D. B. Lover

Since the start of the year, Drouin had been acquainting her
students with allegory, fable, tragedy, the poetry of Milton and
Donne. She'd been encouraging creativity, but not with a rigid
hand; like Dave's seventh-grade teacher, Drouin allowed lati-
tude in essays. "What you think is certainly as important as
what I think," she said, "believe it or not!"
    As part of her teaching on the differences among romanti-
cism, realism, and naturalism, Drouin asked her class to write
three essays. Students would pick a topic and interpret it three
ways: romantically, naturally, and realistically. They would
work in small groups, each to produce one set of essays. With
few exceptions, their topics were violent. Class secretary Missy
Beauchamp wrote about being blown up by a mine, Matt
Stone about a monk who raped a woman, Dave about a zom-
bie. Another boy described a female English teacher being
drawn and quartered.
    "I've never had a class that responded with such joy to may-

hem," Drouin said. "You kids frighten me, I have to tell you. What is it? Hasn't anyone ever let you go before?"

Extreme violence came from a group of girls—cheerful, pretty girls who played sports, had boyfriends, and were well liked. Their naturalistic essay was about a severely abused boy who slaughters his parents; along the bottom, they wrote: "Ideas taken from *Faces of Death Part I*," first in a series of five videos, including the "Worst Of" volume, which show uncensored footage of electrocutions, hangings, maulings, and similarly gruesome deaths. The girls' romantic essay was on the relationship between Lu and Sarah, the woman Lu loved. "He was a psycho," the essay began, and when he had the chance, he brought her to a cemetery, where he placed her on an altar he'd prepared. "He gagged her, pulled out a dagger and punctured her skin gently, then dug the dagger deep into her flesh until he cut enough to reach her heart. When he did, he reached in with both his hands and ripped out her heart while it was still beating in his hands. Lu then sucked out every ounce of her blood and left her carcass to rot as the steam rose from her once warm body into the cold night air."

"So this is what the Freddy generation is all about," Drouin said. She was referring to Freddy Krueger, villain of the successful *Nightmare on Elm Street* film series; like *Faces of Death*, it was a popular weekend rental in Burrillville.

As the first frost came to southern New England, Dave often wished all his courses were like honors English and Martin's journalism/creative writing. He considered Spanish and physics a waste of time, but at least he could fill those periods with shenanigans and work on *Godhead*. There was no such relief in precalculus; department head Eugene Kenney, a noted disciplinarian, taught the course. And that would have been fine with Dave if he'd liked math, but he didn't anymore. Worse, he stunk. In Algebra 2 the year before, he'd gotten a

76, his lowest final grade in any course since freshman year, when he received a 72—for Algebra I. Kenney was a good teacher, but he could have been speaking Chinese for all Dave understood. Having scored a 37 on one quiz, he was in danger of flunking.

From friends, Dave was getting reports of great goings-on in World Lit. Drouin was lecturing on heroes and asking her kids to remember their dreams so they could discuss them the next day. They were reading Lovecraft and Poe and watching a film about Joseph Campbell, the mythologist. No one would be so nerdy as to put it this way, but what was best was how they were learning about each other, and themselves.

Even Drouin was tugging Dave, albeit gently. "You belong here," she said.

"I know," he answered. If only his mother agreed.

A hunter's moon rose on Monday, October 19, the first day of Spirit Week.

Spirit Week was one of Burrillville High's great festive traditions, ostensibly intended to pump up the football team for Saturday's homecoming game, but really an excuse to have a last bit of fun before winter set in. Monday was Pajama Day, and while he came to school appropriately dressed, Dave was more intent on Spam. Capitalizing on the previous week's publicity, the *Godhead*ers had proclaimed Spam Week, and Dave and Brian went around school passing out bite-size samples from a silver tray. Tuesday was Invisible Day—teachers were at a conference, students were off—and Dave and Beth went with Gene to Boston's Museum of Science, where the headliner was a *Star Trek* exhibit. Wednesday was Clash Day: Kids wore mismatched clothes and, coincidentally, attended an assembly on conflict resolution (Narrator: "Too often when we face conflicts, we'd like to punch their lights out, rather than calmly settling differences"). On Thursday, Dave, dressed in a tuxedo and wearing Mickey Mouse suspenders, emceed Mister Bronco Night, an evening-long affair that included a talent show and a swimsuit contest, which drew wolf whistles and wild applause from the girls. The winner was Justin Laferrier, a red-headed senior who played football and lifted weights.

By Friday, the high school was pulsating with energy. You could feel it the first minute of first period, in honors English. Drouin ordinarily had the power to control with a look, but this morning the power was gone.

"I'm used to attentive audiences," Drouin said. "All eyes on me."

"Wait—one of my eyes has a cataract!" Dave said.

"I'm not dancing, I'm not singing, I'm not teaching until everyone is quiet," Drouin said.

"I like this!" said Scott Bridge, who sat next to Dave.

By lunchtime, 11:28 A.M., low blood sugar was a factor. For over an hour, kids had watched the clock, and when the buzzer finally sounded, they bolted. Down the corridors they surged, a shouting, elbowing, frenzied crowd of kids, each determined to be first in line.

Even under ordinary circumstances, lunch was an adventure in control. Except for immediately before and after school, when everyone was rushing off somewhere and didn't have the chance to enter the mob-psychology mode, lunch was the only time in the school day that kids were together in such large and random numbers. Because of limited seating, the lunch hour was actually three shifts, each with nearly three hundred boys and girls from all four classes. Each was presided over by assistant principal Lee Malbon—Doc, as teachers and students alike referred to him. Doc carried a walkie-talkie and was assisted by two teachers, whose charge was not so much enforcing etiquette as heading off chaos.

Dave had second lunch. Moving fast or cutting, which he'd developed into an art, he usually got to the head of the line. When he emerged, his tray invariably had an extra brownie or carton of milk, stolen or sweet-talked out of a sympathetic worker. Then it was over to his table, where he had exactly twenty-three minutes to eat. Dave did not sit just anywhere; no one did. Through some silent but irrepressible instinct, kids had sorted themselves the very first day of school: in crowd girls at this table over here, in crowd boys at the table next to them, honors girls over there by the wall, losers and silent types consigned to the fringes. Most students at the tables were of the same gender and grade, and all obeyed the pecking order: underclassmen on one side of the room, upperclassmen on the other. As surely as graduation was in June, you started your high school career on one side of the lunch hall and ended it on the other.

Joel, Gene, Matt Leveille, and Bridge sat at Dave's table, which was between jocks and in-crowd girls. Joining them was a freshman Gene had nicknamed Lyle because somehow the name fit (Fred, his first choice, somehow didn't).

Lyle was a quiet kid, an easy target for punks. Lyle ate alone the first few days of school. Head down, mute, he would move through the line and take a seat at a table near Dave's, even after Gene had christened him and there was no place to hide. "Lyle!" a *Godhead*er would shout. "Lyle! Lyle!" the rest would join in. You just couldn't look at him without shouting it! But the joke quickly wore thin. After a week, Gene walked over and presented Lyle with a cookie, which he called a "peace offering." The next day, he asked Lyle to sit at their table. Not long after, the *Godhead*ers decided Lyle needed their protection. Whenever they found out somebody had it in for him, they rose to his defense. They tracked down kids who'd taken shots at Lyle and threatened to wrap them in Saran Wrap or hang them from the gym rafters the next time there was trouble. "We need to build his confidence," Gene said, and so they made his seat permanent. They lined up dates for him, convinced him to join Dead Poets, and offered to manage his campaign should he decide to run for class president, which he didn't. They became such a mantle that Drouin worried what would become of him next year, when he would be on his own.

All week, the two tables had skirmished. Doc would turn his back and one of those awful-tasting green beans would fly. Turn again, and limp pasta would be returned. Back and forth, all week, juniors against seniors, until by that Friday of Spirit Week everyone knew a historic clash was inevitable.

"There's tension in the air," Matt Leveille said. "You could cut it." Lunch was almost over. Blood sugar was back up.

A minute later, a crust of bread went airborne. A potato puff came whistling back. Carrots were launched. A cookie. An open can of soda, spun so that its contents flared behind it like a Chinese firework.

"Food fight!" someone yelled.

Doc started toward the upperclassmen side of the hall, but he was too late. Kids were on their feet.

"Food fight!" they screamed.

The whole lunch hall was standing. Dave and Gene joined in, and now four dozen kids, mostly boys, were actively involved. Leftover steak-and-cheese grinders flew, along with macaroni salad, napkins, cutlery, opened cartons of milk, soda cans, anything they could get their hands on—everything but trays and chairs, which had been the heavy artillery in storied food fights of old. Doc watched, momentarily helpless, but not blind. When the bell rang some thirty seconds later and the participants melted into the safety of the back-to-class surge, he had a good idea who they were.

Grumbling, the janitors got busy with brooms and mops. Doc called Chief on his walkie-talkie. When Chief arrived, the color drained from his face; his jaw was set and his eyes were burning.

"I'm going to cancel the pep rally," he declared.

Richard Polacek, math teacher and student council adviser, tried calming him. There was only one pep rally each fall at Burrillville High, Polacek reasoned; was it fair to penalize every student for the misbehavior of a few? What message would that send the spectators—and the kids, two thirds of the school, who weren't even there? What kind of lasting bitterness might be engendered? Chief listened, and even in his anger, he knew Polacek made sense.

"I want the class officers to meet me in my office," Chief said. "We're going to take back control of the school."

Rumors always sped through Burrillville High, but none traveled faster that fall than those about the pep rally. Chief had barely opened his mouth, it seemed, when the entire school knew something was up: *The pep rally's canceled.* Come on, dude, get real. *Honest to God—it's true!* They can't do that. *Wanna bet? I've never seen Chief so bullshit!* They cancel the pep rally and there'll be a walkout, just wait and see!

Dave had returned to Spanish, where one of the perpetrators, a boy named Jay, was re-creating the fight in detail. When their teacher said they'd be lucky now to have the rally, Dave snuck back to the cafeteria, where he found Chief surveying the mess.

"I heard the pep rally is canceled," Dave said.

"It's an option under active consideration," Chief said.

Dave scooted off. He had to find Michaelman, class president, to see if he had any brilliant ideas on how they might save the day. Dave wasn't the only one scrambling. Marcy Coleman, student council president, and Jodie Cooke, council vice president, had already talked to Polacek, who suggested they make their case directly to Chief. Polacek had his own strategy. He marched Jay back to the cafeteria, where Chief had stern words for him.

Sixteen class officers could not fit comfortably into the principal's office, so they were shepherded into a conference room in the guidance suite across the hall. The silence was like the *Godhead* meeting with Chief. The senior officers tried, with some success, to act cool, but the freshmen were visibly terrified.

"Maybe I shouldn't be here," Dave whispered.

"Maybe not," Michaelman agreed. "Chief's wicked pissed." By the time Chief arrived, Dave was gone. No sense putting your ass on the line without good reason.

As Mitchell saw it, education had gotten vastly more complicated in the quarter century since his first job, in 1969, as a teacher in York, Maine.

By the time he became Burrillville High's principal, in 1990, kids were growing up in a culture unimagined twenty-one years before. Violence, date rape, child abuse, alcoholism, addiction, divorce, teenage pregnancy, the influence of ever-more sophisticated media on impressionable young minds— the litany was disturbing, if all too familiar. It seemed that an increasing number of parents expected more of educators than they did of themselves, that a new and stingier economy had become an enemy of parents who still slogged away. It seemed that lawyers had reached into the classroom and choked off some of the learning, that politicians saw schools as little more than whipping posts for society's ills (but damned if they were going to get one more taxpaying dollar to get the job done). Sometimes it seemed to Mitchell that discovery and the pursuit of knowledge, two of childhood's treasures, had gotten lost somewhere. It was easy to believe that any kid who made it through adolescence intact today was some sort of miracle. Mitchell kept coming back to respect, the fundamental lesson of his own growing up. The Penobscots in the 1950s were no longer slaughtered, but socially and economically they remained deprived of dignity.

"The place is a pig pen in there," Chief said to the kids in the guidance conference room.

They could not look him in the eye.

"I am not happy, to say the least. My instinctive reaction is to cancel the rally."

Chief was silent a moment before explaining his displeasure. "The need for respect for one another—that's number one for me," he finally said. "This type of action does not represent that. That's not what we're about. I'm angry—very angry. But before I make a decision, I want to talk to you. I need your input. I need your advice. I need your help."

Krissy Remington, vice president of the senior class, spoke first. She was one of the strongest personalities in the class of '93: class president freshman and sophomore years, vice president junior year, captain of the varsity cross country and girls' basketball teams—a girl who had the respect of her peers, though some of them, jealous, gave it grudgingly. Krissy volunteered time to help disadvantaged kids, and she'd cofounded a home-cleaning business. You expected no less from a Remington. Remingtons had come to coastal Rhode Island from England in the 1600s, inland in the early 1800s. They were merchants, and their continuing prosperity could be seen in the lumber business Krissy's father, Clinton O. Remington III, a state representative, successfully operated.

Krissy acknowledged how wrong the food fight had been, but didn't believe that should obscure the issue of fairness. At most, she said, 5 percent of the student body had been active combatants.

"I don't think the other ninety-five percent should be punished," she said. "It would be a real big damper on Spirit Week."

"What do you think we could do in the future to address these sorts of issues—in a positive way?" Chief asked.

All agreed: Punish the perpetrators.

"Have them clean out the cafeteria," Krissy said. "Do that for a week. I think that would teach them a lesson."

Polacek came into the room with four boys, including Jay, who was struggling to suppress a grin.

"We have some participants who would like to apologize for their actions, if that would help," Polacek said.

"It's certainly a start," Chief said.

"We'd like to apologize," said senior Mark Wojcicki, a soccer and tennis player whose ambition, as spelled out in the yearbook, was to be like Sam Malone, bartender on *Cheers.* "We know it was a stupid thing and we overreacted."

Chief sent the boys to the cafeteria to help the janitors. Then he addressed the class presidents: "If we go ahead with this rally, will you four class officers join me on the floor and talk about this?"

Gladly, they said.

"This is your school," Chief said. "Don't ever forget it. It's not my school—it's your school. Take good care of it."

The homecoming dance was that night in the cafeteria, cleansed of all traces of the food fight. Chaperones were at the door, taking money and turning away kids on the suspension or academic ineligibility list. Doc and two policemen kept their usual high profile. There were no fights inside, as sometimes happened, and only two confrontations in the parking lot afterward, including one between a senior and a middle-school kid who'd drunkenly taken on all comers. The senior won. The fight would be one of the hot stories at next Monday morning's weekend wrap-up, but not the hottest. The hottest were almost always about sex.

Dave arrived at seven, when only underclassmen were on hand and the four-hundred-dollar deejay was still running sound checks. When no one was looking, Dave went to a side door and let Beth in. She was not supposed to be here; like most dances, this was open only to Burrillville High students, who presumably would be less trouble than strangers from out of town. Dave snuck Beth to the back of the lunch hall, to darkness and the relative safety of a screened-off area used for the culinary arts program.

"Until more people get here, you better stay here," he said. "If Doc sees you, he'll throw you out."

"I'll chill," she said.

Beth was too young to claim charisma, but she had undeniable presence. Boys' heads turned when she walked by. Girls talked about her behind her back. They noticed her clothes. They noticed her hair. It was naturally blond, given extraordinary bulk and height through the application of chemicals that came from cans. Beth liked mirrors. She had green eyes, flawless porcelain skin, and perfect cover-girl features, but at that phase of her life, the eve of her fifteenth birthday, she forsook nature for makeup.

"Like, what are you gonna do?" Beth said.

"See if I can get D. B. Lover to come out."

"Think she's here?"

"We'll see."

As Beth chewed gum and talked to a girl that Justin Mc-Gale, Dave's friend, had snuck in, Dave disappeared into the crowd. Seven-thirty and the cafeteria was filling up. Hockey season would soon begin, and when it did, dances would be in hiatus until spring because nothing could compete with hockey in Burrillville on a Friday night. Dave made his way toward the front, where some *Godhead*ers were. So far, everything seemed ordinary. Seniors had the middle of the floor, the in crowd the core of that. Underclassmen mostly strolled or stood in clumps along the walls. The deejay was playing with his laser and smoke machine. No one seemed intoxicated, but Dave was sure several had been drinking or smoking marijuana, or both; red eyes and the sickly sweet smell of Double Bubble over booze gave them away.

Dave was an outstanding dancer whose imitation of Michael Jackson always drew a crowd, and on any other night he would have been dancing by now—with Beth, or some of the senior boys who, like him, were into stage diving, slam dancing, and rap. Girls might not admit it, but these guys were better than most of them.

In the past week, Dave had shown D. B. Lover's letters around. "This is psycho" was Gene's reaction. "No one in his right mind types this bad. This is strange. This is whacked. This is seriously insane." As evidence, he noted the atrocious typing and all the words that had been underlined or crossed out. The scariest touch was the jagged heart D. B. Lover had drawn at the end of one letter. It looked like Freddy Krueger had signed it.

"Some of this stuff could be fake," said Michaelman.

"No, this is definitely real," Gene said. "It mentions stuff you'd only know if you were really watching. This is definitely someone keeping an eye on Dave."

"This is a girl," said Kelly O'Rourke.

"What if it's a guy?" said Gene. "It doesn't say anywhere in here that it's a girl."

Identifying D. B. Lover had become Dave's obsession. In the days ahead, when he got nowhere on his own, he would show the letters to his father, who would ask the postmaster to trace them. He would show them to Chief, who would conduct his own investigation and inform the police when they came to school on another matter. But for now, Dave was going to handle this on his own. He'd smoke that sicko out— all he needed was a plan!

He had several. Maybe he'd start a false rumor that he and Beth had broken up and see if that flushed D. B. Lover out. Or pretend to be flattered—publish an invitation for a secret rendezvous in the next *Godhead*. Tonight, he would appear to be alone—available. Tonight, he was bait.

No one bit.

Beth was as disappointed as Dave. "Was a little pissed cuz D. B. Lover didn't make an appearance," she wrote in her diary. "She's gettin' beat when I find out who she is."

Dave was less upset at D. B. Lover not materializing than he was at Doc. Doc was not the kind of administrator every kid warmed to, but he had no illusions about that; he was the guy who broke up fights, handed out suspensions, and took water pistols away from kids like Dave. He'd taken punches in his years at Burrillville High, and he'd faced down kids cops could barely handle. He knew every troublemaker in town and the circumstances, usually traceable to the family, that had made him that way. He'd stuck by enough kids to have learned that with patience and hard work, young lives really could be straightened out. That, Doc claimed, was his reward.

This counted for nothing with Dave, who despised Doc's

latest law-and-order campaign, directed against the unauthorized wearing of hats on school grounds. Didn't Doc have anything better to do than confiscate caps? It wasn't as if they were packing handguns or dealing acid in the boys' room, for crying out loud. And wasn't there a constitutional issue here? If you could legally burn a flag, why couldn't you wear a Bulls cap in school? But what ticked Dave off tonight was how quickly Doc had zeroed in on Beth: less than an hour to pick her out of a crowd of over two hundred. After lecturing Dave, Doc ordered him to take his girlfriend home. Dave did, but not before asking for his money back at the door. He got it: five dollars for him, five for Beth. Considering that he'd snuck Beth in and he'd slipped past the chaperones without paying himself, it was all profit.

"Doctor Malbon wouldn't allow Beth to stay at the dance, but about 801 million other visitors were there," Dave wrote in his diary. "At least I made $10 out of it. Ha, ha, ha, Doc!"

But the last laugh would be on Dave, for it would be his continuing anger at Doc that would help provoke the conflict ahead.

▲ *Dave and Beth at a sports awards banquet.*

Chapter 5

BETH

*"Adults are like, oh, it's only puppy love or she'll grow out
of it, ya know. I'd love to spend the rest of my life with you."*

—BETH SUNN, IN A LETTER TO DAVE

The five dozen kids at the Bettencourts' were mostly friends of
Dan. He'd just finished eighth grade, would join his big
brother next fall at Burrillville High, and tonight was his annual pool party. Paul and Leslie were circulating. Boys were in
the driveway, shooting hoops. Girls had congregated on the
deck, where soda and snacks were being served. It was July 10,
the summer before Dave's senior year.

Beth stood out from the moment she was dropped off. It
was the way she made her entrance—as if she expected everyone to notice her, which they did. It was how she didn't really
mingle with the girls. It was her look. She wore boy's shoes,
yellow trousers, and a Cross Colours T-shirt with the slogan
PEACE IN ALL THE HOOD. She had bloodred lipstick and rings
on every finger. Pinned to her fly was a blue condom on a lollipop stick, a novelty item she'd found at a gag shop. Beth was

into rap. And no one at Dan Bettencourt's party was out there with her.

"Who's that?" Dave asked Jay LaForge, his friend. They were the deejays.

"I don't know," Jay said.

"That's Mrs. Sunn's daughter," Dan said. An English teacher at Burrillville Middle School, Ruth Sunn's passions were bird-watching and books.

"No way," Dave said.

"I'm serious," Dan said. "I saw her at a dance."

"You like that look?" Jay said.

"Yeah," Dave said. "But it's kind of ghettoish. I mean, I bet she dates black guys." If she did, Dave figured, she wouldn't have much interest in him. He was standing there in shorts, kerchief, and official Olympic Dream Team basketball shirt. Cool, but more Bird than Barkley.

After a saunter around the pool, Beth stopped at the deejay booth.

"What is this shit?" she said.

"R.E.M.," Jay said.

"Why aren't you, like, playing rap?"

"We'll play rap later," Jay said.

Beth wandered off to talk to her friend, a classmate of Dan's who'd told her about the party. Damn, she was good-looking. Too bad she hadn't brought her bathing suit! Dave would have put money on her having a super figure.

And didn't this screw things up—Lauren Raspallo, the girl he still had feelings for, was here tonight, too! She and Dave had gone out about a month, until, one afternoon in the spring, she called. They chitchatted like they always did, and then, pretty much out of nowhere, Lauren gave him the line no one ever forgets: "I just want to be friends." She hoped Dave understood because, well, it wasn't like they'd been engaged or anything, and now he could go out with other girls, and no matter what happened he was a really great guy, and blah-blah-blah. Dave was angry and at the same time wanted to cry, but all he could do was hope that someday, she'd realize how wrong she'd been . . . and maybe want him back.

So he couldn't come on to Beth, not with Lauren around, but what harm could there be in a few words? On their break, Dave and Jay went looking for Beth.

"Here we go," Paul said to Leslie. They'd noticed Beth, too. She looked like a serious walk on the wild side.

"You're Mrs. Sunn's daughter," Dave said.

"Yeah," said Beth.

Dave pointed to her condom and said: "I like that—do you think I could jump through it or something?"

Beth laughed.

"No, really—can't I just jump through it?"

Beth laughed again. She already thought Dave was cute and now she knew he was funny, too. And older—old enough to drive! Too bad she'd heard, wrongly, that he was still involved with someone. Beth would never ask a guy out, that wasn't cool, but there was no problem flirting.

Beth was intelligent and analytical—a girl whose style, sometimes mistaken for conceit, was to assess new situations before making a move. She wore contact lenses, and as darkness had fallen she'd had to squint to get a fix on this crowd, mostly kids she'd never met because she was from out of town. Watching her, one girl became convinced she was giving dirty looks. When Beth turned, the girl threw two cookies at her.

Beth spun around. "Look," she said, "if you're gonna throw cookies at me, come step."

"You got a problem, why don't you solve it," the cookie thrower said.

"Come on, let's start it," Beth said. "Right here, right now."
Beth had never been in a fight in her life. She was five-three
and weighed 105 pounds.

"Sorry, no blacks allowed at this party," the other girl said.

" 'Scuse me, you fucking racist!" Beth yelled.

Beth and the girl were moving toward each other when
Dave stepped between.

"There's nothing to see here!" he said, mimicking a cop at
the scene of a crime.

"Yo, that's whack," Beth said. "She's racist!"

"Nothing to see! Keep on moving!"

After the party, Jay and Dave got to talking about Beth.
"You ought to ask her out," Jay said. He would have himself, if
he didn't already have a girlfriend.

"Yeah, but what about Lauren?"

"It's over with Lauren," Jay said.

"I don't know . . ."

"Come on," Jay said. "You guys could come out with Nikki
and me. We'll go to the movies."

Sunn was an Anglicization of Beausoleil, French for "beautiful
sun." Beth's great-great-great grandmother, a Connecticut
Yankee named Caroline Ames Medberry, had insisted Joseph
Napoleon Beausoleil drop it before she'd accept his proposal of
marriage. The Sunns had prospered, and subsequent genera-
tions had been comfortable, but not prolific. Beth's father,
Tim, was the last male in the line.

A student assistance counselor, Tim had charted a zigzag
course through school, preferring cars and sports to scholastics
until well into college, when a dean he respected put it on the
line: Shape up or get out. Middle-aged now, he was still a mo-
torhead, still a jock—into tennis and no-check hockey and rac-
ing his black '61 Corvette, which he'd modified to do zero to

sixty in 3.2 seconds. Ruth was the academic of the family, a private, intense woman who taught writing to seventh-graders, a daunting but rewarding vocation.

Bethany Ruth Sunn, their only child, was born on November 2, 1977. She was a restless baby, curious to the point of self-harm. Beth would escape from her stroller and climb out of her crib, once sustaining a cut on her chin that took eleven stitches to close. She brushed her teeth with Ben-Gay because she liked its smell. She ate holly berries and Flintstone vitamin pills and drank a bottle of liquid Tylenol after chewing off the cap. Things were so bad that her pediatrician advised Ruth to stock up on ipecac, a purgative. Ruth was glad she did.

One winter when she was two, Beth wanted to go barefoot in the snow.

"No, Bethany," Ruth said.

"I want out in the snow!"

"No, Bethany, your feet will freeze."

"I want out!"

Ruth relented, with the predictable result: Beth's feet soon were scarlet.

Beth screamed. "My feet hurt!"

"Now do you understand why you can't go out in the snow?" Ruth said.

One day when she was thirteen, Beth and a friend had a major brainstorm: They would go for a joyride. God, it would be cool! It would blow their eighth-grade friends away! Beth knew where to get the wheels: next to her father's barn. There, alongside Tim's Corvette and the parts to a '32 Ford he'd bought when he was fourteen, was a 1980 Honda Civic. It was nothing fancy, but it ran and had a sticker and a license plate. When Ruth wasn't looking, Beth could slip the key off her ring and away they'd go.

Except on the first try, she took the door key, not the key to the ignition. Well, next time they'd get it right. They'd wait for a curriculum day in the North Smithfield school system, when students had the day off. The night before, Beth's friend would sleep over. When Tim and Ruth left for work the next morning, they'd put on extra makeup in an attempt to look older. They'd find a gas can so they could refuel without having to drive into a filling station, where one wrong move could bring catastrophe. Away they'd go, windows down and radio blasting.

"Imagine if we get caught." Beth said the night before.

"I'd be screwed," her friend said.

"No kidding. So would I."

"We're not going to get caught."

"No way."

The next morning, Beth was on her best behavior. As Ruth and Tim got ready to leave, she and her friend showered, made their own breakfast, cleared the table, sat down, and opened their books.

"What are you guys doing?" Tim said.

"Studying."

That's weird, Tim thought, Beth studying—and at this hour! But what was he going to do—convene an inquisition? Sometimes, you had to have faith.

When the Sunns had left, Beth and her friend went out to the Honda. Beth was afraid she'd hit the barn backing out, so she put the transmission in neutral and they pushed it clear of the building. Then they got in, Beth at the wheel, her friend beside her. Beth started the engine. The Honda had a stick shift, but she'd seen her daddy work one often enough to understand the basic principle.

Backing out of the driveway, Beth drove into woods.

"Shit!"

"You're not driving," her friend said and took the wheel, somehow managing to get them free.

"I can do this," the friend said.

"Yeah, you're pretty good."

The only thing she couldn't master was the clutch, but that was no biggie. Whenever they wanted to stop, Beth's friend simply shut off the ignition. Starting up in gear was tricky, but after the bucking stopped, you were under way.

Their first destination was the home of another girl; as they waited for her to get ready, Beth walked over to a gas station and, with some of the six dollars she and her friend scraped together, filled the jug. They went to McDonald's next and then to a drugstore for hair spray—parking in an open area of the lot both times so they wouldn't have to back up. By late morning, they were in Woonsocket, next to North Smithfield. They were taking side streets to Mount St. Charles, a Catholic prep school where Beth had more friends.

"Holy crap! I can't believe you did it!" they said.

"Yeah, we did it," Beth said, in her ultimate-cool voice.

Now there were five girls in Tim and Ruth's Honda—five early adolescent girls, laughing and carrying on so hard this fine June morning that they couldn't stop the tears.

The police cruiser was coming toward them—headed in the opposite direction on this two-lane road.

"The cops!"

"Oh, shit!"

The three girls in back ducked. Beth's friend floored it and the Honda blew past the cruiser. What a close call! Were they ever lucky today! Beth looked in the mirror. The cop had turned around. He was behind them now, getting closer.

"It's over, guys," Beth said.

Maybe not! Maybe they still had a chance! Maybe it would be like in the movies! Beth's friend ran a stop sign—the first girl's home was just ahead. The Honda turned up the drive. The girls were on their way into the house, trying to act as if nothing was going on, when the cruiser pulled in behind.

"Excuse me, ladies, where you going?" the cop said.

"Inside."

"Who was driving?"

"I was," Beth's friend said. "Kind of."

"Can I see your license and registration?"

"Ah, I don't have a license or registration," the friend said. Everyone but Beth started to cry.

Tim was at work at Woonsocket High School when the call came in. "Do you have a daughter named Bethany Sunn?" the officer said.

"Yes," Tim said. My God, she's been in an accident, he thought.

But the officer sounded businesslike. "Do you own a white 1980 Honda Civic?" he said.

Those little sons of bitches! Tim thought.

Tim drove his pickup to the police station. "I'm sorry," Beth said when he walked in. He wouldn't hear it. He chastised the girls for their stupidity, told Beth's friend she was forever banned from his house, took his daughter and left. "Get in the back of the truck," he said. "I don't want you in the front with me." When they pulled into their drive, he said: "Get the hell in the house."

It hurt, having to treat her like that. Beth had been into dolls and pretty dresses when she was little, but what she really wanted was to be a boy. She had play tools and G.I. Joes, and her favorite outfit was overalls, flannel shirt, and baseball cap, just like Dad. Tim had never been this angry at Beth—so furious that Ruth was afraid he might hit her, which he'd never done. Tim didn't, but he insisted on pressing charges against Beth and her friend, even when the friend's parents tried to talk him out of it. A family court judge handed Beth twenty-five hours of community service and a similar sentence to her friend. (Beth did her time serving meals at a center for the elderly.) Beth was grounded indefinitely, and Tim dropped her from the softball team he coached. For eight days, the only words he had for her concerned consequences, judgment, and truth.

"Do you realize what could have happened?" he said. "If you'd gotten in an accident, we could have lost this house."

"I'm really sorry, Daddy," she said.

"Sorry doesn't cut the crap, honey. We're not doing sorrys right now. That's down the road a bit."

In raising their child, Tim and Ruth had sought a balance between independence and control. Tim's father had been an overbearing, unforgiving man until late in life (when, like some sort of modern-day Saul, he'd become a Christian missionary in the jungles of Brazil). The Sunns were determined not to be like that with their daughter; they wanted a full and rich human being. "Stick up for yourself," Tim told Beth. "Demand respect." But also, he advised, recognize impossible situations. "There are some not-nice people in the world who have control and authority over us," he said, "and sometimes the best thing is to just get through it and move on." It was a philosophy Beth tried to apply at school with teachers who disliked her, a philosophy she would need the year she dated Dave, when a cheerleading advisor gave her grief for wearing the wrong color scrunchee—*the wrong color scrunchee!*—in her hair.

The Sunns believed experience was a worthy teacher. In their ongoing dissection of the joyride, Tim said to Ruth: "It took a lot of courage to do what she did. It took a lot of guts.

It was independence, freedom—I mean, she really did a lot of things we've always encouraged her to do."

"Too bad," Ruth said, "this is how she chose to show it."

On the eighth day, Tim's anger was spent.

"I'm sorry, Daddy," Beth said.

"I was hurt," Tim said.

"I'm really sorry."

"I do not like being lied to. It's important that you and I trust each other. If we don't trust each other, we are nowhere. Now forget it. It's over."

By the time Dave came into her life, Beth was much like him: moving rapidly and in many directions. She was the rapper chick who showed up at Dan's party, a cheerleader, an athlete who played tennis, soccer, and softball. She collected Teddy bears and *Sesame Street* dolls. She shopped. She worshiped with her parents at a Baptist church. She was a *C* student, barely—capable of better but not trying because school bored her, just as it had Tim. She included honor students among her friends, together with a pregnant fifteen-year-old, a girl who'd been abused by an alcoholic father, and a girl whose mother had hung herself. "I think Bethany is a secret voyeur," Ruth said. "She lives vicariously through these dysfunctional lives. She doesn't seem to be very interested in people whose lives are like hers." Except, as it turned out, Dave.

Beth had a potent imagination. In the long run, it undoubtedly would enhance her life, but at fourteen, it was bedeviling. She was terrified that aliens would kidnap her—away in a spaceship to inflict unspeakable horrors—and when she was returned, no one would believe what had happened. Sometimes, lying in bed, her contacts out and the night air rustling the curtains, she would look at her window and a head would pop into view. A head! An oval-shaped head! Her heart would flutter and she would clutch her Big Birds and her Ernie and scream: "Ma! Dad! UFOs!"

She watched TV programs about them, anyway. One that particularly spooked her was about MIBs: Men in Black, who prey on people who have seen UFOs and reported them to the police. "There's been a wicked lot of cases of, like, men in 1970 Cadillacs," Beth explained, "perfect, spotless Cadillacs, and all black suits with black derby hats on who come up to, like, the people's doors and, like, harass them kinda. They have really round faces and squinty eyes—not like Chinese— like, weird eyes, long eyes, and they harass these people! And so they think that's the new thing—like, it's like the aliens coming back to say: 'Don't say anymore,' you know?"

Beth was working at a summer camp at Burrillville High at the time of Dan's party. "Are you in a gang?" this one boy got up the courage to ask. Beth couldn't resist putting him on: One look, and you knew he was such a dweeb.

"Yeah," she said, "I'm in a gang."

"Wow! Where is it?"

"North Providence," Beth said. North Providence, where Paul Bettencourt had grown up, was as tame as a place could be. "It's called the Queen of Hearts. There's a bunch of black girls in it."

The dweeb wanted to know if they carried weapons. Beth said she didn't—but you'd better believe the others did.

"If anyone starts on us," Beth declared, "they get beat down."

What Beth didn't say was that she and her friend Jessica had cooked up the Queen of Hearts one night while watching *Alice in Wonderland.* "I don't lie good," Beth explained, "but I bull-shit good!"

She watched MTV, read *Glamour* and *Cosmopolitan,* and

had subscriptions to *Tennis, Teen, Seventeen, Young & Modern,* and *Episodes,* a soap-opera magazine. "My Boyfriend Slept with My Best Friend" was a cover story in an issue of *Young & Modern.* "My Boyfriend's Best Friend Raped Me" was another. In the first-person "Say Anything" column in one issue, these were among the most mortifying moments submitted by readers: a girl whose father farted in her boyfriend's face, a girl whose tampon clogged a toilet at school, a girl who stuffed her bra with tissues, and a girl who urinated in a pool, allegedly laced with a chemical that turned urine green. Only the urination tale rated four stars, for Ultimate Supremo Humiliation.

Beth believed you were a loser without fashion. You had to ride the wave and, when it broke, climb the next one. She started her freshman year in understated preppie: jeans, button-down shirt, and black leather shoes, a basic Gap look. By winter, she was checking out rap: sneakers, baggy jeans, and hooded sweatshirts, and hair that was poised to ascend. Then it happened. One day, as she was looking through a rap magazine, she saw a picture of Monie Love, a black rapper. Monie was wearing orange Cross Colours overalls, a purple shirt, and a purple-and-orange checkered hat. It was so dope! Beth showed the picture around school and the girls all thought it was so dope, too. And when Cross Colours arrived at the mall, Beth was one of the first to buy them. She was onto the next wave.

Sometimes, Ruth didn't know what to make of her daughter. That rapper look, that rapper attitude and rapper talk—it seemed to have sprung from nowhere; Beth had African-American friends, but they were suburban Rhode Islanders, just like her. That summer, when Ruth was taking a course in the history of the English language, she was tempted to write an essay titled, "My Child Speaks English As a Second Language."

Although she is attractive, a petite woman with golden hair

and delicate features, Ruth never thought of herself as having much appeal to the opposite sex when she was Beth's age. And so it was a new experience, watching her daughter become Narcissus. "You should be a hairdresser so you can look at yourself in the mirror all day," Ruth would joke. "Shut up," Beth would reply. And Ruth would think: She's really pretty, she's everything I always wanted to be. Like Tim, Ruth believed self-expression extended to fashion, but there were limits. Wearing a condom on your fly was unacceptable, and Ruth had ordered Beth to remove it when she was leaving for Dan's party. Beth did—and then, out of her mom's sight, put it back on.

There were many battlegrounds. Beth didn't like to cook, although she knew how. She hated doing laundry and cleaning her room, didn't like to be rushed getting ready to go out. Every morning, Beth and Ruth competed for bathroom time. Their fights were often screaming matches.

"Do the dishes," Ruth said one day.

"I'm not doing 'em," Beth replied.

"Do the dishes, Beth."

"Get out of my fucking face, Mom!"

That did it—that word. Insolence was one thing, obscenity another. Ruth chased Beth upstairs and when she had her cornered, slapped her. Later, calm restored, Beth said: "I didn't think you could run that fast!" They laughed.

Mostly, Ruth surrendered: It would be easier carrying the burden of housework while waiting for adolescence to run its course. "Call me when she's in college," she would say to Tim, who sought refuge in his Corvette.

One afternoon the week after Dan's party, Dave was playing tennis at Burrillville High. He'd been thinking about what Jay had said about Lauren, how he had to close the chapter and move on, when he saw Beth bringing her summer-camp kids over to shoot hoops.

Years ago, Dave and Beth had attended preschool together, but Dave didn't remember her from then. He remembered their second encounter: a trip his fifth-grade class took to Washington, D.C. Ruth Sunn had been one of the chaperones, and she'd brought along her daughter, who was in third grade. Beth had just gotten her first pair of glasses, and Dave thought she looked like a perfect little dork. Boy, has she changed! he thought.

While the kids played, Dave talked with Beth, and it was nice and easy, so he figured, what the heck.

"Jay and his girlfriend are going out Friday night," he said. "Do you want to come? We're going to *Cool World.*"

"Oh, I have a date that night," Beth said.

Well, that was that . . .

"But I'll go out with you anyway."

Beth broke her other date—it was with Ryan Murphy, a hockey star at Mount St. Charles and son of a couple Tim and Ruth knew. Beth and Ryan had gone out twice already, and until Dave, nobody would have been surprised if they had wound up a couple before summer ended.

Dave drove everyone in Leslie's Buick. As they sat in the theater, waiting for the lights to go down, they started busting on a kid who was wearing a blazer and a beret, not cool.

"Like, what the hell is that?" Beth whispered.

"I don't know," said Jay, "but I wish I had an extra-long arm so I could just reach forward and smack it off his head." They all cracked up at that.

The movie—*Cool World,* a cartoon—was no good, but Dave and Beth were comfortable together. Dave shared his candy, and partway through the film, after weighing the odds of acceptance and deciding they were in his favor, he reached for her hand. She'd been sitting there hoping he would. Afterward, they went to a record shop and McDonald's, and then to Round Top fishing area, a secluded hangout on Dave's road. Beer cans, cigarette butts, and condoms were among the trash clean-up crews periodically removed from the Round Top lot.

Jay and his girlfriend went off into the woods, leaving Dave and Beth alone in the car. They kissed. It was cool.

But as they were waiting for Jay and Nikki to return, Dave said: "I just got out of a relationship a little while ago. I think I want to date around for a while."

Stupid retard! Beth thought. What kind of dumb thing is that to say on the first date?

"That's OK," she said. "I had a good time tonight."

"Me too."

The next day, Dave called Beth. And on July 20, ten days after Dan's party, he asked her to go steady. She'd known all along he would.

As September approached, the people around Beth and Dave could see it was going to last.

Paul and Leslie liked Beth the more they got to know her, but sometimes they worried that Dave was too serious with a girl too young. Dave's sister didn't share that view. To Laura, Beth was the real thing: a teenage girl with hip taste in everything. Besides, Dave was Laura's hero. She wore his clothes, laughed at his jokes, had a Michael Jordan poster on her door, and imported his high school lingo to the middle school, where she was an honor-roll student in sixth grade. Dan had less enthusiasm for Beth. Dave was three years older than Dan, and all things considered, he was about as decent a big brother as a kid could want. They shared a bedroom, and ever since he'd gotten his license, Dave had been Dan's wheels. He'd brought Dan into his Dungeons and Dragons circle and always let him play ball with the guys. Dave had never fallen like this for a girl. Dan felt like she'd taken his brother away.

And the guys—they didn't initially embrace Beth, either. She and Jay got along, but early relations with Joel, Matt Leveille, and the rest of the D&D crowd were touchy. No one missed the hickeys Dave brought back from nights with Beth. No one wondered why it was so hard to get through to him on the phone. "Dave's whipped," they whispered. None of them had girlfriends at the moment, although not for lack of desire. Matt especially made no secret of his desire. Son of a banker, Matt was a tall, freckled, friendly boy with a great, if sometimes gross, sense of humor. He played rec league basketball, wrote a sports column for the *Blueprint,* and was always talking about girls. The running joke with Dave and Joel was that it would be easier on everyone if they just chipped in and bought him a mail-order bride for Christmas.

In North Smithfield, Beth was dealing with the same dynamics.

"All my friends are very jealous of you and me," she wrote in a letter to Dave. "Because they said, 'Beth, you are really very happy and you really love Dave because when your with him you have a smile that's so *big* and you look so happy!' Then I'll tell them what we did that past weekend and when you do sweet things for me, like the balloons."

Fun was the primary objective. They sought it in movies, playgrounds, cars, and Dave's room, which had a phone and a small refrigerator always stocked with candy and Coke. They liked the Dream Machine, a video arcade with the newest games: Mortal Kombat, Streetfighter, and the rest. They liked malls, and whenever they went, they bought cookies and checked out the toy stores, and usually Dave paid, although Beth often offered with what was left from her six-dollar allowance. Dave even took his girl to the *Godhead*ers' favorite restaurant: China Pit, they called it, a Chinese restaurant in Woonsocket where the food was cheap and manners optional. Beth was no match for Dave on food. A trip to McDonald's for him was three burgers, large fries, and a shake. Taco Bell was a half dozen tacos. Between meals, he ate potato chips, corn chips, cheese curls, chocolate, pastry, soda, milk, fruit juice—liquid or solid, it made no difference how he got his calories. He always had gum. And yet his weight never budged: 125 pounds throughout his senior year.

One thing Beth and Dave rarely did was party, the favorite weekend activity for kids who were, or wanted to be, cool. It was little wonder that partying was so big in Burrillville. The town may have been heavenly for little kids, but what were you going to do at sixteen on a Friday night—fish? OK, so there was George's Pizza, which had a jukebox and fried foods in great variety. You could drive the Pascoag 500, a loop that took you past George's, Fleet Bank, and the Village IGA parking lot, which after hours was a good place to catch a fight. You could go to X-tra Mart for gas or hang out in the high school parking lot—until the cops broke that scene up, which they did every evening, as predictably as the seven o'clock siren. You could go to McDonald's, a few minutes across the border in Uxbridge, Massachusetts, or see if anything was cooking at Round Top. But you could only do so much of that before it all seemed the same. And there was only so much money for movies and the mall.

So you did what grown-ups did: you partied.

There was nothing formal about parties: The principle requirements were alcohol and a house where Mom and Dad were away, an exception being those rare parents who let their kids drink. Even without groovy sixties folks like that, getting booze was not exactly like prospecting for gold. You either knew which clerks at which package stores were easy on IDs, or had a brother or sister over twenty-one, or were in the good graces of a classmate who'd taken the express train through puberty. Beer, wine, and wine coolers were big at parties, with hard stuff sometimes brought in by somebody in search of high-octane kicks. Marijuana was sometimes smoked, cocaine or LSD occasionally used. Kids often got rowdy, but most times, damage was only spillage and broken glass.

But things could get out of hand. Boys with too much to drink sometimes got into fights. Kids sometimes stole money, CDs, or clothing, even food. On one memorable night, a gas grill disappeared from a cheerleader's house—and didn't surface until the Christmas assembly, when it was the surprise prop in one of the most popular skits. And then there was the party the night of the homecoming game—a party that took its place in school legend with the food fight. The host was a nice boy from a nice family, and his parents were away that Columbus Day weekend—out of state on one of the few vacations they'd taken in more than two decades of marriage. "Party at my house Saturday night," the boy said, and that's all it had taken: an invitation to a few kids, who told a few more, who told a few more still, until everyone knew where the action was going to be that holiday weekend. When it was over, lamps and a telephone had been broken, a mirror smashed, holes punched in walls, posters stolen. Kids had thrown up, passed out, and left the party to do the Pascoag 500 while seeing double. The boy's parents went stratospheric when they got home, grounding their son and demanding restitution. For a few days, he walked around Burrillville High with a box labeled, CONTRIBUTIONS. HELP ME REBUILD MY HOUSE.

Dave's parents were not teetotalers—they sometimes had a glass of beer or wine—and it was through them that their son had been introduced to alcohol: a sip of champagne at a New Year's Eve party. I don't like the taste, Dave thought. Nor did he like the taste of wine, beer, or mixed drinks, all of which he'd sampled over the years. In tenth grade, he'd gone to a party with some basketball buddies and they'd gotten loaded while he drank Sprite tinged with beer, which gave the approximate tint and smell of booze—he didn't want to look like a wimp! By senior year, Dave no longer cared who knew he hated the stuff or what they thought of him for it. He'd seen enough drinkers lose control to know it wasn't what he wanted. Alcohol in moderation was OK, but once most kids— plenty of adults, too—started drinking, moderation no longer existed. Before long, somebody was puking and somebody else was bumping into walls. Kids were slurring their words, often to laughter, a reaction inexplicable to Dave. Normally easygoing boys and girls turned into pressure cookers.

Once after a hockey game, a grown man mistook Dave for someone else. "Jimmy, I'm gonna kill you," the guy said. He stunk of whiskey and Dave got the clear impression he intended to bash his brains out.

"I don't know what you're talking about," Dave said.

"You took my money. I'm gonna kill you!" he shouted.

"What are you talking about? I'm Dave! I'm a little kid!"

But the worst thing about booze, Dave thought, was how it could affect the libido.

On Saturday, September 19, the eve of Dave and Beth's two-month anniversary, Dave was on the deli counter at Li'l General, the convenience store in Harrisville where he worked a few hours a week. Beth had gone to a party where, contrary to what she'd told her parents, alcohol would be served. When Dave got through, at ten, he went to pick her up.

What he found was a bunch of kids drinking in back of a girl's house. It wasn't any dainty wine-tasting, either, but a bacchanalia of beer, malt liquor, Jack Daniel's, peach schnappes, appleberry schnappes, and a grape-tasting concoction called Purple Passion. Cops were called. They gave chase. Beth and Dave managed to get away, but the incident rattled him. It cropped up in *Godhead 2* when Joel, aka the Insipid Utopian, slammed drinkers. It was on Dave's mind for months. And it very nearly led him to dumping Beth.

Like her boyfriend, Beth did not smoke, drink, or do drugs, but even to attend a party where the aim was getting hammered—Dave was beside himself. How could she do this to him? How? In June, he'd been to a drinking party hosted by a member of the class of '92. Several kids had puked and two boys nearly got into a fistfight; but worst of all was a girl who'd come to the party without her boyfriend and proceeded to go into a bedroom with another guy. Didn't they have any decency? It would have been one thing if the incident was unprecedented, but it wasn't. You heard stories like that every Monday morning at school. Dave's nightmare was that some drunk would go after Beth.

After escaping the cops, Dave took Beth directly home. He wouldn't listen to anything she had to say.

The next morning, she called. "I'm sorry," she said.

"I don't want to talk about it now," Dave said.

When he called Beth back, he accepted her apology. That afternoon, he bought Beth a half-dozen red roses for their two-month anniversary. She gave him a Batman toy.

"I guess it must be love!" Dave announced the next day in Spanish, as he showed off his gift.

▲ *The class of '93 poses for its yearbook shot. Gene is center, Dave behind him.*

Chapter 6

THE TURTLE INCIDENT

*"If you can choose things in your life that make you happy,
that don't harm someone else, then that's a big chunk of
successful living."*

—MARY LEE DROUIN

"I'm thinking about dropping precalc," Dave said to his mother one evening as the first quarter of senior year was drawing to a close.

Here we go again, Leslie thought.

"David, there's no way you're dropping that course to take some other course that's not as demanding," she said.

"But, Ma, I hate it," Dave said. And, he added, he was getting a *C*. In truth, he was in danger of flunking.

When she looked back, as she frequently did that fall, Leslie began to recognize—with some surprise—that all along there was her plan . . . and then there was Dave's. Hers held that he would be a good student, active in school affairs, and accomplished in a sport, and that he would go to college, where he'd major in science or engineering. It wasn't an improbable plan; critical parts of it were already realized. Dave had won science fairs and his grades, except lately in math, were good. He played basketball, was on the yearbook staff, and wrote for the *Blueprint.*

Adolescence had brought changes, but they'd been the predictable ones. Dave had gone through puberty, and the physical developments had prompted some teasing by various relatives, including Leslie and Paul. He started dating, and by the time he got his license, shortly after his sixteenth birthday, he was less interested in being with his family. He still vacationed with them, in California and Canada, among other places, but now he was more eager to take camping trips with just his friends. None of this need interfere with her plan, Leslie believed. Having spent a career in their midst, adolescents were not a mystery to her. She knew they rarely took the straight path going anywhere.

But Dave, this kid obsessed with his underground newspaper—who'd fought all fall to get rid of math, who'd set being voted class clown as one of his major goals for senior year, whose school shenanigans Mindy Ryan had made a point of mentioning to her—he hadn't come from nowhere, had he? Leslie had just glossed over the clues.

She remembered many years ago, when she'd tried to steer Dave toward track, a sport she thought suited him; how he'd insisted on baseball, soccer, and basketball . . . anything but track. She remembered how Paul, an Eagle Scout by Dave's age, had tried unsuccessfully to interest him in Scouting. She remembered her own adolescence, how she'd gone to lengths not to be noticed—and now she had this son who, like her father, like some turn-of-the-century vaudevillian, craved the limelight. She knew how easy math was for her and how Dave was honestly struggling in precalc. She knew how much trouble she had with writing and how naturally it came to her firstborn. She knew all these things . . . and still she wondered.

"I want to take another English course," Dave said.

"Why another English course?"

" 'Cause I want to be a writer."

"I think they specialize too soon sometimes in high school," Leslie said. "I want you to come out of there with the basics."

Leslie wasn't being unreasonable: Objectively, the path Dave was taking posed substantial risk of failure. She didn't know of any cliché about starving scientists, but there was one about starving writers, wasn't there. What guarantee was there that he could make it in sports broadcasting or stand-up comedy? What if he got into college and decided science and math were what he wanted after all? No one could predict the future. It was the same rationale she'd applied when Dave wanted to quit Sunday school before being confirmed. But that was two years ago. Dave was different now, not so easily persuaded.

"I think you should keep all of your options open," she said.

"No more math for me," Dave said. Leslie knew this time he wasn't backing down.

Once again, Dave laid it out: how the course he wanted to take instead of precalculus was demanding, an investment, and taught by the most incredible teacher at Burrillville High. How this was one decision he could promise her he'd never regret.

And on that evening, Leslie finally said the words Dave had been dying to hear: "Do what you want."

The next day, he withdrew from precalc, with a grade of passing.

One morning in October, word went out over the PA that the senior-class yearbook shot was about to be taken. Dave and the *Godhead* crew feverishly began making *Total Godhead* signs, which they brought to the gym along with plastic pistols and a fake Uzi, hidden in backpacks. More than any other photograph, this would capture the spirit of their class. They weren't about to blow it. There was only one yearbook they'd be bringing to reunions.

Ernie LaTorre, English teacher and school photographer, was setting up his equipment when Mindy Ryan walked into the gym. Ryan had a sense of humor, but not for guns or *Godhead.*

"Put them away," she ordered.

The signs and guns disappeared.

Ryan walked back to LaTorre.

The guns and signs went up.

Arms folded, Ryan stared.

The guns and signs disappeared.

LaTorre started taking pictures.

"Cote's pointing a gun at the wall," Ryan said. Someone had a middle finger up. Someone else was doing rabbit ears behind someone's head.

This time, LaTorre spoke. All photographs were closely scrutinized, he said, and anything "bizarre or unusual" would be sanitized during editing. They knew it was true. In their junior class shot, they'd held up a Slayer sign, which had been airbrushed away before last year's yearbook had gone to press. He needed a few more takes, but LaTorre got the shot Ryan wanted.

LaTorre was one of Burrillville High's free spirits, a fortyish man who wore sunglasses and kept his jet-black hair long. He had biting humor and he spoke his mind, which earned credit with kids but not always with superiors. LaTorre believed American education had been slowly sterilized by politicians, administrators, and lawyers since he started at Burrillville High, in 1969. "It's ideas that frighten them," he said.

LaTorre was adviser in 1984, when a two-page section titled "On the Lighter Side" was published in the yearbook. A pic-

ture of LaTorre was there, with the caption: PORTRAIT OF A
PSYCHOTIC PATIENT WITHOUT HIS MEDICATION. But the photo
that caused the rumpus was of a male teacher seated near a female student. GET YOUR HAND OFF MY KNEE, MISS, the caption
said. The teacher wrote letters, threatened a lawsuit, and demanded the yearbook be recalled. LaTorre insisted the caption, written by a student, was innocent. Didn't anyone have a
sense of humor anymore? The American Civil Liberties Union
came to LaTorre's defense, and when tempers had cooled, he
was retained as adviser. To those who found those captions
shocking, LaTorre told the story of a private school in Providence, whose yearbook a few years before had contained a picture of the lacrosse team: If you looked closely, you could see
that one of the players was displaying his penis.

"More and more a yearbook is seen as a tool for public relations," LaTorre said on the day of the class of '93 shoot. "It's
all a game."

In Ryan's eyes, a serious one. She remembered the LaTorre
controversy. She'd had a similar experience herself the previous
spring over a three-paragraph story on the bottom of page
sixty-three of the 1992 yearbook. Written by Jodie Cooke, last
year's underclassman editor and this year's co-editor-in-chief,
the piece described how kids feel leaving the middle school for
high school. "According to those interviewed," Cooke wrote,
"the middle school did not adequately prepare them for high
school." It seemed innocent—what lower-level school *could*
prepare fourteen-year-olds for a world ruled by the likes of
Dave?—but when the yearbook appeared, during budget de-
liberations, no one seemed to have that perspective. To quell
the outrage, Ryan sent a letter of apology to the middle school
principal, Bob Morissette, who was fiercely protective of his
students, his reputation, and his school.

"This goes out to the community," Ryan explained as the
class of '93 left the gym. "If it goes out with a kid pointing a

gun at another kid—even if it's a toy gun—we're going to have all kinds of calls to the principal."

"I'm so glad it's our picture," Dave said as he brushed past Ryan.

That night, he expressed his sentiments for her in his diary: "Get a life," he wrote, but he didn't drop it there.

"Lately, as I stood back from my perch and observed the senior portrait," Terry Gimpell wrote in the lead story for *Godhead 3*, "I noticed that a certain authoritative figure disallowed signs to be in the picture. The signs, not malicious or libelous, were highly creative . . . not all yearbooks have to be straight-laced, boring pieces of information. . . . Maybe the students were making a statement: They don't want to be just another bunch of seniors. What is wrong with that? If the yearbook is going to be a dictatorship, maybe we should start boycotting it."

In other matters, Dave was showing restraint as he put together the third issue of his underground newspaper. The attacks on the in crowd were history—geez, there was one bunch that couldn't take a joke!—and the language was cleaner. The *Godhead*ers had gotten their wish: A few kids had mailed in quarters for home subscriptions, and several had written letters. Some were commentaries on serious issues of the day, and Dave slotted them in. But others were unbelievably gross; they made *Godhead 1* and *Godhead 2* look like choirboy material. The grossest was by a writer who called himself the Wet Rim Rider, or Perv. Wet Rim Rider had a penis complex. He hated women. He was preoccupied with feces. He was a goddamn mess, but whoever he was, he wanted *Godhead* to print his songs. "All the girls are shuten down, I never get no pussy," one of them went. "The only action in my pants has been a fart." Another bemoaned impotence—his own or someone else's, one could only guess. "Always limp from alcohol," that song went, "it's a small, small dick."

There's some real sick puppies out there, Dave thought.

Few were as sick as D. B. Lover, who'd followed the initial two letters with obscene phone calls to Dave and Beth (the voice sounded female, but it could have been disguised), a letter to Beth, and four more to Dave. The menacing undertones of the first communications had been replaced by an overt hostility that was alarming, especially in light of other developments that fall. Starting with the turtle incident, northern Rhode Island seemed to have entered some strange new karmic zone in which anything bad was possible.

The turtle incident began one morning when Richard Toomey's photography class went into the wetlands adjoining Burrillville High on a nature shoot. Michaelman found a baby turtle and brought it back to school with the idea that Cote would tape it to his cap, which was his billboard, always crowded with buttons, pins, doodles, and proclamations of all sorts. The turtle was still around at lunch. Brian Ross saw it and was struck with inspiration. He would pay twenty dollars to anyone who stood on a table and bit its head off! Twenty dollars—one chomp! Brian expected no takers; except for Ozzy Osbourne, no one could be that sick. This was a put-on, folks! This was for laughs! One kid took the animal in his hand and, imagining the taste of turtle blood, quickly declined. Others wouldn't touch it. The episode seemed to be over, when a boy not known for brainpower picked the turtle up. Twenty bucks? Twenty bucks was decent change! The boy put the animal in his mouth, gently clenched, and attempted to decapitate it by stretching the neck. It would not give. Damn, turtle meat was tough. Only one thing to do: bite hard. That worked. The boy spit the pulsating part onto a tray, and as the cafeteria recoiled in horror, he asked for his twenty bucks. Chief moved immediately on this one, calling the police and animal control officer, and suspending the boy, who did not get his twenty dollars, since he'd neglected to stand on the table.

But most of the violence that fall was directed against humans. In Woonsocket, police still sought the youths behind a series of beatings and threats, and, in a separate incident, arrested three high school freshmen for shooting a nine-year-old boy with a high-powered BB rifle as he played outside at recess. Worst was the shooting death of a twenty-year-old man in North Smithfield, Beth's town, during a party over Thanksgiving weekend. The alleged murderers were sixteen and seventeen, kids turned killers in a drunken dispute involving a girl. They were arrested two days later in Indiana after allegedly committing two armed robberies in Connecticut and attempting a third in Ohio.

"Your girlfriend is just Miss Social, isn't she?" one of D. B. Lover's latest letters declared.

"She walks around and guys are literally drooling over her and girls all smile at her and I don't even think thier jealous of her. It amazes me that somone doesn't hate her bad like me . . . I can't wait to see her at the dance. You never know David, something just might happen there." D. B. Lover called Beth a "black wannabe" and other racist slurs.

> P.S. I found out that she was a cheerleader recently. Oh my god I almost died. She is one of the most popular people in our school. (SHE DOES NOT EVEN COME HERE.) Plus she is a cheerleader. I will throw up soon . . . Damn, I wish I was your lover. You are so hot if i type anymore I'll get wet . . . love you lots and want you bad.
> I LOVE YOU 4-EVA

Was it a put-on? Could anyone's sense of humor be that fucked up? Dave didn't think this was a joke, not after reading the letter Beth received. "Believe me, I am watching you when ever you are in Burrillville," D. B. Lover wrote, "no matter where you are." Written across the top of that letter in a deranged hand were three words: "Die, Die, Die."

This was seriously sick shit. Dave didn't advertise it, but in light of his recent roughing-up, D. B. Lover's latest had him on edge. He didn't really believe D. B. Lover would do anything, neither did Beth, but what if? That was the scariest part. What if D. B. Lover had a knife? A gun? D. B. Lover could be anyone, anyone at all. . . .

Beth's parents downplayed the letters' significance—nothing would be gained by making their daughter paranoid—but privately, they were concerned. They supported Paul Bettencourt's effort to have the postal service track down D. B. Lover, and Chief's notifying the police. Publicly, Dave, Beth, the *Godhead*ers, and a growing number of students who'd caught wind of what was up were irate. There was nothing in the latest correspondences to help determine if D. B. Lover was psychotic or just some loser kid perilously close to a breakdown, but distinctions didn't matter anymore. The consensus was that they should find, and punish, the perpetrator.

Maybe D. B. Lover found out what they had in mind, because nothing happened at the next dance, on Friday, the thirteenth of November. Dave didn't let go. "Message for Miss Lover," he wrote for *Godhead 3*. "Your notes are not fair. Please give me a return address so I can respond. Terry."

Recent graduates of Burrillville High were excelling at Harvard, Smith, Brown, Boston University, and many fine state universities. They were at community colleges and had careers in theater and film. Several had served in Desert Storm. Still others were waiting tables, delivering mail, or banging nails. A few were in prison. It was both the challenge and the strength of public education, diversity.

World Lit was as good a mirror of Burrillville High as any class. Valedictorian Marcy Coleman, who planned to study chemistry at Brown University, was enrolled, along with the class poet, Rebecca Courtemanche. So was Justin Dawes, an old friend of Dave's who played three sports, loved the Beastie Boys, and pierced his own ears. Michelle Bynum, an artist and daughter of one of the janitors, was in World Lit, together with Krissy Remington and TammyLyn Dupuis, who'd all but raised her younger brother and sister when her parents divorced and her mother went back to school. Gene wasn't officially enrolled, but he often snuck out of his English class to attend.

With half the enrollment of honors English, Drouin could teach in large groups, small groups, or one-on-one, depending on the subject and mood of the day. She could more easily stage plays or radio skits, or have the class sing or dance. She could move everyone outside in good weather or into the B-wing hall when the weather was bad and her room, cheerful as it was, had become the same old place. Her biggest constraint was the bell. Drouin gladly would have ripped up the daily schedule—seven periods, each precisely forty-six minutes long —if she could.

By the time Dave arrived in World Lit, Drouin had finished with several weeks of horror fiction (her Dead Poets Society had gone to Providence for a performance of *Dracula*) and moved on to heroes.

"There is a traditional code of values we tend to apply to folks who are heroes," she said. "Violating it can make you a villain." And one person's hero, she explained, may be another's villain. She gave as an example the Pilgrims, traditional heroes to whites, but not to Chief's people.

Drouin asked her students to go to the board and draw up their own lists. For historical characters, good and bad, they named Columbus, Hitler, Gandhi, and King. Contemporary characters included Bush, Schwarzkopf, Spike Lee, Madonna, Anita Hill, Clarence Thomas, Magic Johnson, Hillary Rodham Clinton, and Joseph Mollicone, a Rhode Islander whose banking crimes precipitated a statewide crisis. There were no African-Americans taking World Lit, but nearly half the heroes the class named were black. Dave chose Malcolm X, Dawes Jackie Robinson, the first black player in major-league baseball. "Jackie took unimaginable punishment from the white-dominated society," Dawes wrote, "but he always stayed with his code of honor, and knew that he was making the world a better place." Dave enthusiastically agreed.

As Drouin saw how obviously Dave enjoyed his new class, she sometimes thought about his mother. Drouin knew Leslie only by reputation and what she'd read in the paper about her science prizes and grants. That was enough to know that Dave dropping math for writing couldn't have been easy. For Leslie, a part of the dream must have gone.

Even if she's personally disappointed, Drouin thought, in the larger sense she must be thrilled to have such a really sweet, talented, nice child. I know I'm happy for him. Because in the context of high school, this was a big thing to do.

WINTER

▲ *Dave runs the Bronco offense.*

Chapter 7

BRONCOS

"Success is never final. Failure is never fatal."

—COACH JOHN WIGNOT

The Boston Celtics were Don Ferry's team. He bought into the leprechauns, Red Auerbach's cigar, the ghosts of basketball giants peering down from the rafters of that ancient edifice, the Boston Garden, where so many banners hung. If summer was Red Sox, winter was salvation. Don had been there through the great years, the Russell, Cousy, and Havlicek years, and during the period of decline he'd waited patiently, confident that unlike those bums across town, Celtic greatness again was only a matter of time. His patience was rewarded. In 1979, Larry Bird was drafted, and within two seasons he'd helped capture the first of three championships that would be Boston's in the 1980s. By 1986, when Dave was in fifth grade, Bird and Magic Johnson dominated the NBA, and it was their appeal, talent, and presence on TV that were turning basketball into an internationally marketed commodity.

Dave was visiting his grandparents that April afternoon in 1986 when the Celtics were defeating the Chicago Bulls in the first round of the playoffs. The game was on TV. Bird scored thirty-six points and had twelve rebounds and eight assists, and on some other day, his performance would have been the highlight clip on the evening news. But this was not some other day. A new kid, Michael Jordan, was setting an NBA record: sixty-three points in a playoff game, all the more extraordinary considering that the day before, he'd scored forty-nine.

Dave was thunderstruck.

It wasn't just the sixty-three points—one guy! half an entire team's production!—it was how Jordan got them, with jump shots, three-pointers, dunks, and buckets from the line. It was the way he mesmerized—a graceful athlete who had perfected movement like no one Dave had ever seen. It seemed that if he wanted to, Michael Jordan could fly.

Nobody can stop him, Dave thought. He's awesome!

It was in some ways curious, Dave and sports. Neither Leslie nor Paul had passion for athletics, and they hadn't pushed their son onto the playing field, didn't believe his development would be stunted if he didn't someday captain a team. But ever since he was a toddler, Dave had been fascinated with sports: baseball, football, tennis, lacrosse, even golf and candlepin bowling. Any sport, so long as it was on TV.

Before Dave was born, Leslie had a student named David. He was a scholar and track star, and Leslie was sufficiently impressed with him that he was, in part, the inspiration for her son's name. But her Dave wanted nothing to do with track. Like, what was the point? So you ran around—big deal. Dave played Little League baseball, but he was small and it seemed to Leslie that big kids and coaches' kids got the most playing time. The Bettencourts assumed Dave's sport would be soccer, second in Burrillville only to hockey, of no interest to Dave since he didn't like skating. Parents ran the soccer leagues. They drafted the players, worked the concession stands, and organized the fund-raisers and awards ceremonies, when everyone on every team got a ribbon or trophy and a round of applause. Weekends, parents would fill the water bottles, pack the lawn chairs into the minivans, and bring their sons and daughters to the soccer fields, which were surrounded by trees. Sitting there under the wide-open sky, you could track the change of seasons in the leaves.

Dave excelled at soccer. He was fast, his reflexes were quick, and his size wasn't inhibiting. On this course, he would start for the Burrillville High varsity, a perennial power. Except that at the beginning of fifth grade, Dave discovered basketball.

This was more like it! You could play basketball anywhere. You didn't need the ruggedness football demanded, yet basketball was no sport for wimps. There was constant scoring, which made for constant excitement, but you almost never got so far behind that a game-of-the-week kind of comeback was out of reach. Basketball was his grandfather's sport. Basketball was—well, it was just better than soccer, and it was always on TV. And when bedtime came, you could secretly tune your bedside radio to whatever game was on tonight.

If you were lucky, it was Michael Jordan's Chicago Bulls.

Don Ferry was one of eight children. At seventeen, the world at war, he dropped out of high school to join the navy as a ship's cook. When peace came, he returned to Rhode Island and took a job in a warehouse for a grocery chain. Don was a redheaded young man, handsome and strong, and that was one reason a secretary named Dolores DiSimone was attracted to him. Another was his personality. Don was a storyteller with a flair for the limelight. Not that Dolores's folks thought he was anything special—he was just another mick without a diploma. In the 1940s, Italians were coming into their own in Rhode Island. The DiSimones owned property and had been to college, and one of them, Dolores's brother, was an MD—a surgeon, no less. They would embrace their Irish son-in-law, but it would take time. And children. And on Don's part, success.

He went up through the ranks, packing boxes, cutting meat, and running departments before reaching the front office of the Star Market Co., one of New England's large chains. The Ferrys had six children, and Don supplemented his income with his nightclub act and work as an auxiliary policeman. Eventually, he earned a high school equivalency degree. He was a state representative for ten years, a Democrat who served as chairman of the House Finance Committee. In 1986, he ran for Congress, unsuccessfully. Don's campaign consumed him that year, but seeing his grandson's infatuation with Michael Jordan, he found time to buy Dave a backboard, which Paul put up in their drive.

Don had always been soft on Dave. During his grandson's *Sha Na Na* days, he would take hat and cane and perform along with Dave. He did card tricks and magically pulled quarters from behind Dave's ear. He took Dave fishing, treated him to ice cream, played hide-and-seek, sat him on his lap and told stories about manning the big guns as Japanese kamikaze fighters came in wave after wave. Dave was on Papa's softball team, whose archenemy was Dave's uncle's team. Don gave Dave one of his treasures: an Impossible Dream team mug, commemorating the 1967 season, when the Red Sox almost won it all.

Don told jokes. His favorite, which Dave did not hear until he was older, concerned a man whose nephew has a speech impediment. The man goes to the manager of a Kmart and says his nephew is the best salesman in the world—but no one will give him a job because of how he talks. OK, the manager says, I'll give him a shot. The nephew gets assigned to sports, and before long, sales are up 50 percent. The manager can't believe it. How's he do it? he wonders. To find out, he hides in the back of the sports department one day. A customer comes in. Speech impediment and all, the nephew talks him into buying a fishing pole. But wait—now he's selling him tackle! And a boat! And a motor for the boat! And a trailer! Jesus, that's incredible! the manager tells the nephew when the customer's gone—he came in for a fishing pole and he bought all this stuff! He didn't come in for a fishing pole, the nephew says. He was looking for Kotex. I said so long as you're not doing anything for the weekend, you may as well go fishing.

After school, on weekends, after dark under the garage lights, with his friends or Dan, or alone—in the rain and on sun-drenched summer days—Dave shot baskets against the back-board his grandfather gave him. He pretended he was Michael Jordan, or a TV broadcaster doing Jordan play by play. He collected Bulls pennants, Bulls programs, Bulls caps. A friend who made trading cards made a "Dave Jordan" set for Dave. Paul and Leslie bought him Nike sneakers, endorsed by Jordan. Until it was stolen in gym, he had a Jordan jersey. For the rest of elementary school, he wouldn't wear anything that wasn't red or black, the colors of the Bulls.

"You're kind of dark," Leslie would say. "You'd look better in brighter colors."

"No way, Ma," Dave would say.

Once, Leslie bought him a pair of green trousers. They hung in his closet until he'd outgrown them.

"What have you got in black?" Leslie would say to department-store clerks.

Dave wanted to be a pro, and he figured with hard work and luck he'd make it. After reading about a college player who drank iced tea saturated with sugar to provide extra energy for games, he started eating raw sugar and drinking soda before he practiced or played. Dave was average height for his age, and on an annual checkup, he asked his pediatrician how tall he was going to get. "Six feet, around there," the doctor said. Rats! Michael Jordan was six-five! The only six-footers who played pro were point guards. Dave made that his position.

In his first year in organized basketball, the town youth league, Dave was named Most Improved Player. In eighth grade, he made the junior high intramural team. He made junior varsity as a freshman, varsity as a junior, but he didn't start. Coach Wignot saw him as unspectacular but dependable, his strengths desire and a thorough knowledge of the game.

A week of basketball tryouts began the Friday before Thanksgiving. Football players were excused until after their Thanksgiving Day season finale, but all other candidates were required to be at every session. Some forty boys sought twenty-five spots: thirteen on varsity and twelve on JV, numbers determined not by the league, but by Burrillville High's budget. Many of the hopefuls were freshmen, including one who was pudgy and short. Only fantasy could have possessed him to walk under the unflinching lights of the Burrillville High gym, the Bronco Dome, where his huffing and puffing were an embarrassment to everyone but him.

After the last tryout, Wignot and assistant coach David Marcotte struggled with the makeup of their team well into the night. They'd known at the end of last year who most of their varsity players would be, but not all, and it was selecting the last two or three that confounded them at this late hour. Finally, they decided.

In fourteen years of coaching, Wignot had never found a good way to announce the final roster. He knew of coaches who brought the candidates one by one behind closed doors to disclose the decision, but he'd never done that; he could imagine that scene, all in a cold sweat as they waited to be called. No, Wignot did what most do: He turned on his computer and typed up the list. At seven o'clock the next morning, he posted it near Chief's office. Within minutes, boys were coming by to check. Dave didn't bother. Leaving the gym last night, Wignot had pulled him aside and said: "Make sure you're here at two o'clock to get your damn varsity uniform!" Wignot knew there was a place for Dave. He just didn't know where yet.

The dreamers—it was over for them. Outwardly emotionless, they stood at the bulletin board, reading the list again and again, on the crazy chance that somehow they'd missed their names. Emotionless still, they faded away into the pre-homeroom mob. There was always wrestling . . . and for everyone but the seniors, next year.

Besides Dave, Scott Bridge was on the list. So was Kevin Blanchette, this year's captain. And another of Drouin's honors English students: Jonathan Brooks, an All-State musician. Colin Brady, the kid Dave wanted to room with in college, made the team, as did Jay, one of the instigators of the food fight. And Jeff Fague, founder of Minority Street Posse. Off court, Jeff had been in trouble much of his junior year, but it hadn't affected his performance on the JV team. Wignot saw a hard-working kid with talent and determination, and he had a gut feeling that Jeff could be turned around. The scuttlebutt this year suggested he'd been right.

One name was conspicuously absent.

Like Dave, Justin Dawes was funny and creative. He wrote poems. Sometimes he wore fingernail polish, and he'd pierced his own ears. His wardrobe featured bowling shoes, a Kmart vest, John Lennon sunglasses, and a plaid work shirt that had come home from a party minus a pocket and a sleeve; fearing the washer would further shred it, he rarely laundered it. Dawes's dad, a conservative fellow, didn't quite know what to do with his youngest son. "Are you trying to make a statement?" he'd ask. "Jesus, Mary, and Joseph!"

Dawes believed a boy should do something with his body as well as his brain. He was another of Burrillville High's natural athletes, a tall, strong kid filled with an itchy energy. He was on the varsity football team three years. He pitched and played right field for varsity baseball, and, on a vote of his teammates, would receive the Sportsmanship Award his senior year. He made JV basketball as a freshman, varsity the next two years.

Wignot did not dislike Dawes or doubt his talent, but he questioned whether he would stay focused for the entire season, whether he would hurt or help the team. Whatever he decided, he knew, somebody would be unhappy. "I hate cutting," Wignot said, and in soccer, with twice the players, he'd never had to. Once, budgets had allowed Wignot to keep more than twenty-five players on his basketball teams, but he'd learned a lesson. "In the years we had twenty-eight," he said, "they were just never happy. If you cut them, they'll hate you for a couple of weeks and then forget about it, but if you keep them and don't play them, they hate you for the whole season."

Dawes was late to school December 1, and in his rush to get to class, did not check the list. He didn't see the need. So sure had he been of making the team that when yearbook biography forms had been passed around earlier that fall, he'd written: "Basketball, 1, 2, 3, 4." When friends broke the news, Dawes thought they were putting him on.

In January, the hurt was still there. Dawes put his feelings in a letter written in the third person. He showed it to Drouin, who said no purpose would be served sending it to Wignot or circulating it around the school. He took her advice. "Justin, like the rest of the football players, had one day to try out," he'd written. "Unfortunately, he had a bad practice and had to pay the consequences. He had a one-shot deal and lost. No makeups, no second try, nothing. His bags were packed and he went home with no complaints. The humiliation he faced when he went home was unimaginable."

In its season opener, Burrillville lost to Woonsocket, 47–45. Dave was first off the bench. He blocked several shots and had two assists, but didn't get a basket. He scored four points in the Broncos' second game, a loss to Mount St. Charles. Games three and four were losses. On December 11, Burrillville got its first win, against Smithfield. "We've got the monkey off our back," Wignot said. A blizzard that closed school for three days canceled the December 15 game.

The Broncos won their next one, lost the one after that, then closed the calendar year two days before Christmas with a 54–50 win over Exeter–West Greenwich, perennial patsies. Wignot was not a screamer, but he was not the silent type, either. "You're sleepwalking out there," he said at the end of the first quarter, when the game was tied, "you better turn it around now!" At halftime, he turned philosophical. "If all the little parts do their job," he said, "the big part will come together. You have to have faith in each other."

Burrillville had only one bonafide star: Kevin Blanchette, a deadly outside shooter who averaged nearly twenty points a game and thrived in clutch time. Two players, Dan Goodier and Jon Armstrong, had promise, but they were sophomores, in need of experience before they could be counted on. Colin Brady was naturally talented, but he was in only his second year of organized ball. The rest of the Broncos were like Dave: more dedicated than skilled. This was not a finesse team, and before the season began, Wignot expected, at best, a .500 year. Even to get there, he knew the Broncos would have to play their best for the full thirty-two minutes of every game.

Despite their start, the Broncos ended 1992 with a 3–2 record in Rhode Island Class C league play. When the bus pulled out of the frozen Burrillville High lot for the hour ride to Barrington, first opponent of the New Year, Wignot was optimistic. It was January 5.

It would be difficult to exaggerate the distance between Barrington and Burrillville. Barrington was a community on the eastern shore of Narragansett Bay, where America's Cup yachts were built and where, in Newport, Vanderbilts and Astors had put up mansions with rooms too numerous to count; the largest structures in land-locked Burrillville were old mills and a former sanitorium. Barrington had a yacht club, Burrillville the K of C. Barrington's per-capita income was double Burrillville's. If the communities had a great similarity, it was that both had experienced tragedy. Burrillville still mourned its five teenage sons killed in the 1982 car crash. Barrington's pain was more fresh. As 1993 began, residents were bracing for the trial of a man accused (and ultimately convicted) of the 1991 murders of a churchgoing couple and their eight-year-old daughter. Prosecutors said Christopher J. Hightower strangled the mother, killed the father with a crossbow, and buried their daughter, probably alive, on top of her parents' corpses in a grave he dug in a field.

—

No Bronco would have admitted it, but merely walking into Barrington High, home of the Eagles, was intimidating. The high school had a cavernous gymnasium and the home crowd was big. And check out what they wore—down parkas, fancy leather boots, earmuffs, and furs! Only a handful of Burrillville fans and seven Bronco cheerleaders had made the trip across Rhode Island. They looked inconsequential as they climbed into the bleachers on the visitors' side of the gym.

As they dressed, Wignot reminded his team that Burrillville had been listed twentieth in the state this morning by *The Providence Journal-Bulletin,* the statewide paper. The Top 20 was compiled by a single columnist, but his weekly ranking was nonetheless followed closely. And Barrington hadn't made it! "You have a reputation to live up to now," Wignot said. "A team like Barrington might get pumped up for a chance to pick us off."

Burrillville scored first but trailed 20–6 midway through the second quarter. Barrington was, indeed, pumped up, while Burrillville wasn't playing at the level of pickup ball. Nothing would fall for the Broncos—nothing from in close, no foul shots, not even easy layups. Their passing, never strong, was pathetic. On a timeout, Wignot put his chalk down, looked up from his gameboard, and said: "You've got to concentrate on what you're doing. Nothing else I can draw you here." As half-time neared, the Broncos' deficit had widened to twenty-one.

In the locker room, Dave and his teammates sat, heads down, as Marcotte had at them. "I think what you guys need to do is kick yourselves in the ass," he said. "This is a long bus ride to come down here for, a long bus ride to go back." But, he added, there was a way to win: make up nine points in the third, ten in the fourth, and victory would be theirs. "It's not impossible," he said, "unless you believe it is."

Wignot continued on that theme. He'd seen what the Broncos could do when they believed—how their swarming, relentless pressure could confuse opponents to the point where their play broke down. That's how they'd made the Top 20. "You just can't turn it on and off like a switch," Wignot said.

The team huddled. "One-two-three, Broncos!" they shouted, and went running out for the second half.

By the middle of the third quarter, they were down by twenty-three. Wignot was as quiet as the January night outside.

And then something happened—some change in chemistry, some sudden injection of adrenaline, some realignment of the planets. All season, it had haunted Wignot—how the Broncos could stink out the joint, then pull together and put on a show. Kevin Blanchette hit a couple of big shots and the layups started to drop, the passes connect, and with two minutes left in the game, the Eagles' lead was down to thirteen. With fifteen seconds left, the Broncos trailed by six, which is how the game ended: a 60–54 loss. Another minute, and they might have won.

"You guys have to quit playing with my mind like this!" Wignot said after the game. "You're like a high school flirt!" He reminded them of the state championships, held at the Providence Civic Center, Rhode Island's largest indoor arena. If they played every game like the fourth quarter of this one, Wignot said, they could contend for the title.

"You guys can do it this year," he said. "The civic center is yours."

But the next two games, both at home, were losses, including a twenty-point blowout to Narragansett, a credible but not invincible team. "I don't have any more speeches," Wignot said. "I'm all out."

Dave took this seriously. He wasn't Terry Gimpell on the

basketball court; he was a zealot who'd devoted thousands of hours over a third of his life to making the varsity team. Nothing compared to the high of a game—the gym, the crowd, the cheerleaders, the tension in the locker room as you dressed, your girlfriend kissing you after the final buzzer, picking up the paper the next morning and seeing your name. Hitting a layup, connecting on a crisp pass, blocking a shot—Dave didn't know how to explain it, really, except this must be how Michael Jordan felt. Dave was no fool. By seventeen, as his growth slowed and he remained shy of six feet, he knew he would never play in the NBA, not even as a benchwarmer for some lowlife team like the Sacramento Kings (who were so bad they were actually cool, which is why he had a Kings backpack). By senior year, Dave's dream had come down to starting for the Broncos. As the games went by, he began to wonder if he would ever realize it.

Often before a game, Dave felt the need to be alone. He would jog down Round Top Road to the fishing area, where, many months before, he'd first kissed Beth. He loved the woods anytime but especially in winter, when you saw animal tracks in the snow and heard ice cracking as night came on and the air grew still. Your mind could wander wherever it would and no one would care, no one would make you take out the trash or ask if your homework was done or tell you what time to be in. Sometimes, Dave imagined he was one of his characters in Dungeons and Dragons.

Other times, he remembered Don Ferry, his Papa.

Ferry wanted to see his first grandchild achieve three milestones: graduate from high school, be accepted into a good college, and start on the varsity basketball team. He'd died, in October 1991, before seeing any of them.

I'm going to dedicate this year to Papa, Dave had decided before the season began.

▲ *Dave speaks to a teacher prior to his performance at Talent Night.*

Chapter 8

WICKED SWEDISH

"Godhead *sucks.*"

—ROB EDDY, CLASS OF '93

If Dave seemed to swagger on Friday, November 6, he could be forgiven. Last week's *Blueprint* had carried an ad for *Godhead 3*—"the next issue is closer than you think," it trumpeted—as well as a letter defending the underground press and an article by Kevin Blanchette annointing *Godhead* the most provocative thing to hit Burrillville High all fall. In her column, co-editor Kris Lamoureux expressed admiration for the way the *Godhead* staff had handled criticism. Dave felt so good about all the hype that he walked around school passing out signed "limited edition" *Godhead 3*s.

Three hundred regular issues had appeared overnight through the regular distribution channels, lockers, and once again kids were talking on their way to homeroom. Dave had published a whimsical piece on pumpkin stealing by English teacher Ken Lyon, and it generated renewed interest among the faculty, many of whom had been convinced that after an issue or two, *Godhead* would fade away. Drouin got a limited edition, as did Chief. *Godhead 2* had been rough in spots, still too crass for his taste, but this one pleased the principal. "The buzz is on and I love it!" Dave wrote in his diary. Three hundred copies were not enough to meet demand, he decided, and Saturday night, while working at Li'l General, he waited until the boss had left and ran off another hundred on the store machine. He was cruising! He was on top of his game!

(But not with Beth. He got through work and drove to Tammy Bonoyer's house, where Beth was supposed to be. She wasn't there. She was out with some Mount St. Charles kids, among them Ryan Murphy, the boy she'd forsaken for Dave. Dave was ripped when Beth showed up at eleven. Of all people, Ryan Murphy! What kind of shit was this! He's just a friend, Beth said, get a grip. You are definitely a person who needs to get a grip! Their argument ended at McDonald's and was forgotten the next day, when they went to the mall, where Dave bought cap guns for both of them.)

Monday brought more talk of *Godhead 3*. What Dave heard, until mid-morning, was nothing but continued praise.

More than either of its predecessors, *Godhead 3* bore his imprint; for one reason or another, most of the *Godhead*ers had been too busy to put much into it. A few contributed articles, but the brunt fell to Dave, Joel, and Jay LaForge, who'd graduated from Burrillville High the year before and was working in a grocery store while deciding his future. There was no locker-room crudity in *Godhead 3*, no listings of funny-sounding anatomical parts, no expletives. Spam replaced hairy gnome scrotums as the in joke. No one was attacked. Along with the humor was discussion of issues, including a letter to the editor complimenting *Godhead* on its stand against racism and an article challenging the fairness of a suspension policy for students who skipped school. Another article questioned the sanity of spending billions for Stealth bombers when the nation was so deeply in debt.

"What the hell is going on in this country?" wrote Uncle Damned, Cote, who would surprise everyone later in the year by deciding to enlist in the navy after graduation.

> Almost everywhere I look I see pain and misery. People in the streets, people losing jobs because freakin' big business people don't give a rat's ass about anyone or anything except profit. It might not happen a lot right here on a large scale as in New York, for example, but I saw someone not too long ago at Lincoln Mall holding a sign that said "Will work for food." Why doesn't the mighty U.S. Government take some of that "defense" money and put it where its really needed. I mean, who the hell is going to attack the U.S., anyway?

But by second period that Monday, the word getting back to Dave was disturbing. Maybe teachers and the principal thought *Godhead 3* was great, but those who counted most, kids, were grumbling it was too tame. The harshest criticism came from fellow *Godhead*ers, who were starting to think, at least to themselves, that Dave had attempted a coup. Wasn't *Godhead* supposed to be a democracy—all for one and one for all? True, by virtue of his energy, marketing instincts, and access to technology, Dave had become first among equals. And that was cool, his writing was good, his software and computer essential, and he definitely had a flair for PR, but now . . . now, it seemed, he wanted more, maybe all. Ferg told Dave he was unhappy that several letters hadn't been published. Michaelman said Gene was considering quitting because *Godhead 3* was so boring. Rumor had it another boy was planning an al-

ternative zine. The details were hush-hush, but this other kid,
whoever he was, was supposedly willing to push the enve-
lope—publish photographs of fellatio or passages from Hitler,
if that's what it took to get a real shitstorm going.

At lunch, all Dave heard were complaints.

"*Godhead* sucks," said Rob Eddy, aka Theodore Grocki III.

"Big-time," said another kid.

"It's lost its edge."

Dave defended the issue, but his defense withered as the day
wore on. He knew how fast things change. He knew he was
losing something vital, an audience, and it alarmed him. To be
flying so high and then, without warning . . .

After lunch, Dave ducked out of Spanish to look for Gene,
whose loss would be a severe, and possibly mortal, blow to
Godhead. Gene was an only child, and physically he'd matured
sooner than most: At seventeen, he passed for twenty-five, a
fact the *Godhead*ers had exploited in their first-issue lampoon
of themselves. "Hello? Why are you still in school?" they'd
written. "You look like you should have graduated in 1977."
Kids envied Gene, for early maturity had brought him friends
and tastes more sophisticated than many of theirs. He knew
students at the Rhode Island School of Design, Rhode Island's
hippest college. He could get into the over-twenty-one clubs
that featured the best new bands. He was an artist, the best
Godhead had.

Gene's early influences were Spiderman, X-Men, and G.I.
Joe, superheroes that led him to Dungeons and Dragons,
Tolkien, and Van Lustbader, whose ninja epics dovetailed
with Gene's obsession with karate. Until Desert Storm, Gene
planned to be an army ranger—to follow his grandfather,
who'd fought in World War II, and his father, who'd been an
army draftsman during Vietnam. He would be a modern-day
warrior, armed with the latest weapons and parachuting into

some foreign trouble spot to save the day! Nightly news clips from Desert Storm, rich with images of dying, put that romantic notion to rest.

But for Drouin, Gene might have missed the potential in his art. No question, his comic characters were good—but a career? Until Drouin, it hadn't occurred to him. Gene never took a Drouin course, but she was his homeroom teacher freshman year. When he gave her one of his watercolors, she not only hung it on her wall, she gave him advice. "You have great potential," she said. "Use it."

Gene lent a certain prestige to *Godhead* that Dave couldn't afford to lose. If he ever wanted to use art, where else could he turn?

Dave found Gene in another class.

"I heard you're going to quit *Godhead*," he said.

"Who said that?"

"Michaelman. Are you?"

"No," Gene said, "but I didn't like *Three*. There wasn't any controversy."

"We're going to have a meeting," Dave said. "This week. We'll get everyone together."

Gene was satisfied.

"We are nice and that's what we get, criticism," Dave said at the end of the day. "All done with the nice-nice. Time to go hard-core." Time to go controversial, a mantra the *Godhead*ers would repeat, over and over, until they got what they wanted.

Dave's first audience was his family, but by now they were predictable and safe. Beth was a loyal fan, but she was one person. As senior year progressed, Dave wanted numbers. *Godhead* gave him those, but a readership was disappointing in critical respects. Some kids still hadn't figured out who was behind

Godhead. Some knew Dave only in name. Dave welcomed compliments after an issue, but they could be days or weeks in coming. He needed instant gratification. He needed a stage, and that fall, Burrillville High provided one.

Like his grandfather, Dave was fearless in front of a crowd. He handled his emcee duties flawlessly on Mister Bronco night, but mere competence was not enough; he had to perform. It was a simple act—dragging a microphone across the floor in imitation of a bowling ball, a gag he'd seen on TV— but it drew gales of laughter and calls for an encore. Dave had the stage again on Talent Night, which featured rock music, lip-synching, and girls in tight outfits. Dave joined the *Godhead*ers for "A Comic Opera," a silly takeoff on *Little Red Riding Hood* consisting of a fake brawl, fake vomiting, and the appearance of *Total Godhead* to save the day; Dave, in dress and bonnet, played the title character. Students appreciated the act, but the teacher-judges ranked it ninth. "We got robbed," Dave said. "At least Miss Ryan wasn't a judge. I would have been hung!"

Talent Night was barely over when Richard Polacek held casting for the Christmas play; Dave wanted, and got, the role of Marcia Brady. TV was another stage, and Dave made his debut shortly before Thanksgiving, when Dick Martin brought his students on a field trip to Rhode Island's public television station. Dave was one of the students asked to record a promotional spot.

"Loosen up, Dave," Matt Leveille said as they waited to tape.

"I don't need any loosening up," Dave said. "I'm not nervous."

The camerawoman began checking the equipment.

"Hold my gum," Dave said to Joel as he settled into a director's chair. Patricia Merry, assignment editor, pointed to Dave's audience: thirty-six students and a teacher.

"Do you mind if they're here?" Merry said.

"Yeah—well, no, if they don't make me laugh."

The camerawoman wired Dave and explained how the TelePrompTer worked. "This is cool," Dave said.

His first run-through was fine, except for his mispronouncing one word.

"See how easy that was?" Merry said.

"Yeah—except for 'chivalrous.' That word's evil."

"You wrote it!"

"I know. Last time I try to write big words."

Dave's delivery on the next run was excellent until he got to "Channel 36," the name of the station. "Since I was little," he said, "knights of the medieval period always tickled my fancy. The mystique and legend behind these chivalrous figures enticed me to study them further. The Channel Six in-school programming series *Castles* has allowed me to . . . MESS UP!" Everyone laughed.

On the next taping, Dave was flawless.

"Autograph!" Joel said when he was done.

Dave was funniest when spontaneous, and it was his unrehearsed performances that began to concern teachers that fall.

With a whistle for sound, Dave did an uncanny imitation of a dentist drilling. "Damn! Hard-to-reach area! Need the superdeepo drill! Open wide! Wider! OK. Spit!" He was always inventing or customizing words and phrases: *waaah*, for crybaby; *twork*, meaning "to hit"; *wicked Swedish*, for anything that wasn't cool. (He also overused many words: *sassy*, which meant fresh, and *queer*, for hopelessly unhip. He said "that hurts the team"—for something gone wrong—so often, you wanted to erase it from his brain.) He never tired of playing Assassination, a game he and Joel invented. The objective of Assassination was simple: Using a Bingo marker, you left pur-

ple splotches on surfaces unsuspecting people might touch.
There was a premium on teachers, but their choicest victim
was Whistle, the middle-aged chief custodian. Whistle roamed
the lunch hall with mop or broom, cracking jokes and mutter-
ing about kids today and what the world was coming to.
Surely as he would find gum stuck to tables when lunch was
done, every day he stopped by the bubbler for a drink. Seeing
him approach, Dave or Joel would beat him there, clandes-
tinely leaving ink on the button as they pretended to drink.
Whistle fell for it every time. On the score sheet they kept, he
led in Confirmed Kills.

Dave was never deliberately cruel with his humor, nor was
he bound by political correctness, as he knew adults were, at
least in public. This was *high school,* after all. You called 'em
like you saw 'em. If someone was a loser, then that's what they
were—a loser. You would never say that to someone's face—
that would be cruel—but when you were with the boys, an occasional poke was cool. Fat kids got whacked, as did clueless
morons and teachers who thought his humor was asinine. One
particular junior who was a groveling *Godhead* wannabe got
whacked; and, every now and then, one of the special-educa-
tion kids—"speds," as they were indelicately known.

Burrillville spent lavishly on special-needs children, and that
was fine with Dave; that was as it should be. Still, there were
times when one of the behaviorally disturbed kids was having a
bad day—a *really* bad day—literally howling and bouncing off
walls and generally disturbing the peace, such as it was in your
ordinary, everyday high school, and you couldn't let it pass.
Stupid speds—didn't they ever shut up? But anyone could be a
sped: a brother, a friend, a teammate. Declaring someone a
sped was not intentional discourtesy to children with special
needs; the word just had a nice ring, that's all. Sometimes no
other word would do, as in this description Dave gave his diary

of a night at work: "A sped-boy came in and ordered three lbs. of liverwurst. Hello? Sphincter? I think no one in the world can eat three lbs. of liverwurst!" In some peculiar way, it was a testimony to the success of mainstreaming that *sped* had entered the vernacular with such wide application.

Someone campaigning for class clown needed more than words, of course, and Dave incorporated action into his shtick. His face was a comic canvas, and the way he had of tearing down a corridor—arms and legs akimbo, people scattering in his wake—brought to mind the slapstick of silent movies. He was a natural mimic, of Michael Jackson, Ross Perot, Bill Clinton, and any character from a Monty Python movie. Inspired by a TV comedian his father brought to his attention, he added Radioactive Elvis—Elvis Presley mutated by nuclear attack—to his retinue. His best imitation was of Ed Grimley, the *Saturday Night Live* character Martin Short popularized in the 1980s. Unannounced, Dave would bolt from his lunch table, hike his pants as high as they could go, hunch over, and sashay from table to table with Grimleyian goofiness on his face. No matter what Dave did, somebody laughed.

Paul and Leslie didn't see everything, but they saw enough to understand new dynamics were coming into play with their son. "He always had a good personality," Paul said, "but it seems like in the last two, maybe three years he's opened up more. I think he finds high school not challenging academically. I mean, he never cracks a book. He doesn't have to. I think in lieu of that it's, like, 'I'm going to be forward and take charge of class and be the comedian.'" Leslie said: "He's a great kid, just, I don't know . . . *different.* You have to understand—I was a nerd, very quiet, didn't want to be noticed. I can't even imagine how he's trying to call attention to himself like this. He's going to take after my father—some genetic throwback or something."

—

Dave was bored by physics and Spanish 3. "Journalism and English are more important to me," he explained. "I doubt I'll take Spanish in college, and if I do, it'll be a sphincter Spanish course. Like Spanish basket weaving or something!"

Spanish was taught by a woman who took her subject seriously, a teacher who had no trouble with kids who behaved tolerably well and had at least a faint desire to learn. She was genuinely interested in her students, but her strength was not in handling characters like Dave. No matter whether she cajoled, reprimanded, or threatened, Dave would not cooperate. Spanish was an opportunity for him—just not for learning. It was a chance to clown, tell jokes, work on *Godhead* articles, and sometimes cheat on exams. Under one pretense or another, he often got up and left. Armed with a forged hall pass and a semiplausible excuse, he wandered the halls or hid out in one of the computer rooms, where he and the *Godhead*ers played computer games: Spanish 4, they called it. Spanish 5 was when Dave, Joel, John Tebow, and Matt Leveille clustered in the back of the room, playing Dungeons and Dragons. Spanish 6, snow sports, lasted but one magnificent day: December 17, when school reopened after the blizzard of December 12. Spanish 6 convened in the quad, where Dave and Tebow built a snowman that Dave finished with two breasts. "Well-built snowman," Tebow said. "Snowwoman," Dave corrected him. "This is the nineties!"

One day the week after Thanksgiving, Dave's Spanish teacher was absent. The substitute was a kindly woman with glasses and gray hair who'd taught school for thirty-seven years before retiring. She got lonely in cold weather—she missed kids—and so, on a fill-in basis, she always came back.

She was at the blackboard when class began.

"May I have your attention, please?" she said.

In back, Dave and the boys were rolling the dice for Dungeons and Dragons.

"Your assignment is on the board," the substitute said.

"Yeah . . . right . . . uh-huh . . . I see where you're coming from . . . " Dave said.

Few plights at Burrillville High were worse than that of the substitute. Pretty young female subs could flourish, but Lord help the older sub, the nerdy-looking sub, or the male sub fresh from college. Kids were forever toying with them, ignoring them, covering for their friends who had skipped class, making up names they tried to get the poor bastard to repeat during roll call (often with surprisingly easy success): Ben Dover, Mike Hunt, Al Kaholic. Of all harrowing situations, none surpassed facing a class with disinterested seniors like Dave.

But this good-hearted woman was determined. She passed out sheets of white paper. Joel took one—to score his game.

"Don't even bother," Dave said when she handed him his. "I'm not going to do it."

"That's up to you," she said. "I'm not here to fight with you."

But the woman couldn't leave them alone.

"Are you guys in this class?" she said.

"It's specialized work," Dave said.

A few minutes later, she was back again.

"Would you put that away and do your work?" she said.

"I am doing work," Dave said.

"We're actually quiet today," Joel said. It was true.

"You ought to be ashamed of yourselves," the substitute said. But shame had ceased to be a factor in Spanish.

A few minutes later, when Dave and the woman exchanged more words, she ordered him to the office. You had to be kidding! In twelve years, three months, and assorted days of formal schooling, Dave had never been thrown out of class. That was for loud-mouthed losers, not someone like him, who'd made walking the fine line a science!

But the substitute wasn't kidding. Mister Smarty-pants was officially being given the boot.

Dave was stunned. He had no contingency plan for this.

Reluctantly, he left—for the guidance office (not the principal's office; she hadn't specified, had she?), where he talked with Ron Brissette, a counselor he respected. Brissette advised Dave to apologize. On his way back to class, Dave stopped to see what Drouin thought. She agreed with Brissette. Like him, she'd been hearing stories lately about Dave's behavior in other classes.

"I'm sorry," Dave said to the substitute. "Can we just leave it here?"

"Yes," she said.

Others had interest in the way Dave's year was unfolding. Mindy Ryan didn't dispute that he could be funny, but there was a time and a place for everything. One day after the yearbook shot, Ryan ran into Dave in the library. She told him that the public nature of his *Godhead 3* comments had been inappropriate; if he had an issue with her, he should have brought it to her privately. They talked again a few weeks later when he blew a deadline for a sports-page layout; a yearbook, she explained, was different from an underground newspaper. And after hearing that Dave had clowned around when La-Torre did the yearbook staff portrait, Ryan, shortly before Christmas, went to the principal. Chief agreed to watch Dave. If that sort of behavior continued into the new year, he'd also have a talk with him.

"Is this how you want to be remembered for your senior year?" said Dick Martin, another teacher who was concerned.

"No," Dave said. "But some of what they think is immaturity is what's funny in high school today."

Perhaps that was true, Martin said, but one of life's truths is that perception often is reality. And the perception by some was that Dave was screwing up—not providing comic relief to a school that needed it, as Terry Gimpell had proclaimed in *Godhead 1*.

Dave also had an encounter with Doc. It emerged from longstanding animosity between a junior and the *Godhead*ers. The junior fancied himself a writer, and while his public posture was that *Godhead* was idiotic, privately he wanted in on the action. The *Godhead*ers were blunt when telling him, repeatedly, to forget it. He seemed to have gotten the message by early December, when a new publication turned up around school.

Two pages long, *The Misguided Shaft* consisted of clips photocopied from a gay newspaper published in Worcester. Some were of ads for telephone sex services, others of dating services for cross-dressers and transsexuals. Several were infographics of gay and lesbian voting patterns. This quote had been lifted from somewhere: "It's very important for Catholics to see that there are people in the church—bishops—who support civil rights for lesbian and gay people, that it's not Catholic to hate or discriminate as Pat Buchanan was a perfect example of." It was hard to tell what *The Misguided Shaft*'s intent was. Except for its name, it didn't slam gays, nor did it advocate homosexuality. It just seemed to be saying: This is how it is, boys and girls, out there in the real world.

No editor was listed for *The Misguided Shaft* and there was no way, looking at it, that the responsible party could be identified. Somehow, the rumor got started that the junior was behind it—and furthermore, he was a bisexual! It was not an identity the underclassman, who was straight, wanted.

Knowing that, Dave couldn't resist a tweak. "Wait till you see the next *Godhead*," he said.

"There better not be anything about me in there," the junior said.

"You'll just have to wait and see," Dave said.

"I mean it," the junior said. The exchange took place in the *Blueprint* office, where Dave was running off copies of one page of *Godhead 4* on a laser printer.

The next day, Doc called Dave over. He'd heard from someone he wouldn't name that Dave had been using school equipment to print *Godhead*—maybe as many as three hundred *Godhead*s! No way, Dave swore. Honest. The underclassman denied being the snitch when Dave confronted him. Nope, wasn't him—it was Kris Lamoureux. But Dave didn't buy that. Kris was too nice.

On December 8, Dave was accepted into the University of Rhode Island. It was the only place he'd applied.

"URI has a communications program that will hopefully allow me to become a journalist or a broadcaster," he'd written in his application essay. "The university is also in my home state, which has allowed me to visit its campus in Kingston on numerous occasions. I liked what I saw in terms of the environment and the campus." What he didn't mention was that attending URI would keep him close to Beth, who would still be in high school the next year.

On paper, Dave was a respectable candidate. He was tenth in his class at the end of junior year, and his SATs totaled 960, which he figured he could bump past 1,000 when he took them again. But lots of applicants to URI had credentials like his. Earlier in the year, when he'd met with guidance chairman William Griffin, Dave had been looking for an edge. He thought *Godhead* might be it.

"I have a secret to tell you," Dave said. "That underground

newspaper that's floating around—I put that out. I was planning on putting that on there."

Griffin, an educator since 1957, couldn't pass on the chance for advice. "I have no problem with the underground newspaper," he said; what he couldn't sanction was personal attacks. "There's very, very little to be gained by chopping someone down. You must remember that if you do, you have to live with them."

Dave said he'd learned that. So how would a college look at his involvement in *Godhead*?

A conservative school would probably frown on it, Griffin said, while one that was liberal might consider it meritorious. "URI has underground newspapers on their campus," he said. "Their representatives would be much more open to that."

Griffin wrote a favorable recommendation, as did Maria Flanagan, who chaired the social studies department, and Martin, who chaired English. "When I think of David Bettencourt, the first words that come to mind are 'bright, enthusiastic, creative, energetic,' " Martin wrote. "Dave is very much like a fledgling waiting to take flight, and anxious to do so."

Early acceptance took Dave out of the college-admissions scramble, one that for others—kids who were indecisive or had dimmer prospects—could become extraordinarily expensive, time-consuming, and, ultimately, heartbreaking. Unless he flunked a course, which seemed an impossibility (he was passing physics and Spanish with above-average grades), his educational future was secure.

So perhaps it was knowing that this would be the last Christmas he would be at home, or the fact that his eighteenth birthday was only two months away—old enough to be drafted!—that turned Dave introspective as the calendar year wound down.

Burrillville High was more than a school he just happened to have attended for three and a half years, wasn't it? he realized. It had become a sort of second home—a family, as Chief liked to consider it. And if he'd made a game of school this semester, at least he knew the rules. The future was another story . . . one with no happy ending guaranteed.

Over the unscheduled vacation that followed the blizzard of December 12, basketball practices and a game were canceled. "When I think about some things I get scared," he said one day when he had unusual free time on his hands. "Like college and stuff, and things after that, the leaving. I'll have to do everything on my own. Here—I'm noticed. But there, I'll be just like a Social Security number."

The pressure on Dave had increased by the evening in December when the *Godhead*ers convened at his house to pull issue four together. That incredible *Godhead* buzz was gone, victim to the disappointment of issue three, and in the past few days, competition had emerged. Could you believe the nerve—first *The Misguided Shaft,* and now, someone *else* honing in on turf *Godhead* owned! This upstart underground paper was the work of freshmen, and it showed. The typography was crude and the humor made Terry Gimpell seem a comic genius. It didn't have a name, only a list entitled: "Really, Really Bad Gifts for Christmas." Some items were a blatant ripoff of *Godhead.* Dave was not flattered. "Wannabes," he said, as if its authors were the vilest form of life on earth.

Once again, Dave sat at his father's computer and everyone gathered behind him: Gene, Cote, Ferg, Michaelman, and Scott Bridge. Joel, who was out with his new girl, was due later.

"We're going to try to be controversial," Michaelman said.

"Every page," Dave vowed.

One of Burrillville High's traditions was seniors writing songs for the Christmas assembly. The lyrics were guarded like national secrets, but this year, one of the *Godhead*ers had stolen a copy. Cote allowed as how printing *them* would cause a ruckus.

"Are we really going to do that?" Dave said.

"It wouldn't bother me if we chickened out," Michaelman said, "but we don't have anything else controversial." Michaelman was one of the producers of the assembly. He knew he'd automatically be fingered as the snitch.

It was a go.

"This one's going to be way over the line," Michaelman said. "They're going to flip out!"

Dave put the lyrics inside. He had a better idea for the front page: Doc. Dave was still irked that Malbon had kicked Beth out of the homecoming dance, and he, like others, was aggravated that the assistant principal hadn't let up on his dumb anti-hat campaign. What really pissed them off was that the administration had granted an exemption to the culinary arts students for their "team" caps.

"Hat-Hater Slays Two Deer," Dave typed.

Everyone liked that. Driving darkened roads, Malbon recently had struck two deer, causing several thousand dollars' damage to his Volvo. A story had been in the local paper, and Doc, who'd been uninjured, had taken a ribbing, not only from kids.

" 'By the *Godhead* staff' and, in parentheses, 'we're all wearing hats,' " Michaelman said.

"How about 'slays two reindeer'?" Dave said.

"Maybe we should have 'Santa pissed,' " said Ferg.

"Yeah, let's have the controversy start from the beginning," Dave said.

" 'Santa pissed'? Where?"

"How about 'Santa's fucking pissed'!"

"That'd be awesome!"

"Controversial!"

But the boys didn't know the details of the deer deaths. Michaelman telephoned his aunt, who kept abreast of local affairs, but she was no help. Gene, who had the deepest voice, offered to call Doc and pretend he was a newspaper reporter writing a follow-up story. But when they couldn't find Doc's number, they gave up on truth.

"Why not say he hit them in the Bronx or something," Gene said, "where you'd never hit a deer."

"I like that idea," Dave said.

"Make it a story like the deer are real people," Gene continued, "and they just got out of someone's party and like Doc hit them and . . ."

Upstairs, Paul and Leslie watched TV. As careful as they'd been in getting to know the *Godhead*ers, the Bettencourts had some misconceptions. They thought the boys were using legitimate means to reproduce the paper, not pirating copies at Li'l General or the machine at one boy's church. They didn't know how angry some at school had been, or how close Dave had come to a beating. At least they'd seen the paper. At Paul's request, Dave had shown his father the first three issues before publication. Paul had judged nothing libelous, although, like Leslie, he'd warned his son about taste. "You don't have to use rotten language to get your message across," Paul had said. "The kids will still read it whether there's swearing in it or not."

Well, there was certainly swearing in *Godhead 4*. As the meeting ended, Dave took his disk and page dummies so Paul wouldn't find them. He did not intend to show anything to Chief, either.

Burrillville High was manic the morning of the Christmas assembly. Today was the last day of school before vacation—six hours, and then eleven days of freedom!—who could concentrate? Students went class to class passing out gifts. Seniors roamed the halls in Santa hats and elf costumes. Gary Briggs sang carols as Matt Stone wheeled him around in a shopping cart.

And *Godhead 4* was out.

Students had been on the lookout for it. For days, Dave and the crew had been pumping up the hype. Yesterday, a flyer had appeared throughout the school:

Jingle Bells
Santa Smells
Two reindeer have been killed.
Total Godhead.
Coming the day before Christmas vacation.
The most controversial issue ever is about to hit this school!
—Printed by the Terry Gimpell for Congress Committee

A close reading of *Godhead 4* disclosed substance. Gimpell, who'd raised himself in rank from Head Chef to Venison Chef, had an article about underground newspapers at Beth's school. "One of them, entitled *Dogma,* was an Anti-Black and Anti-Sematic paper," Gimpell wrote. "Let's just say it didn't go over well with people in Northern land." In another piece, Gimpell challenged the wisdom of sending troops to Somalia. Gimpell also said Bill Clinton was the change America needed: "He moves into the White House and moves out the Ben-Gay and hot water pads to bring in saxaphones and MTV." Writing under his pseudonym, Bernhard Faber, Michaelman recalled Dave's roughing-up and Gene's transformation to Terminator. "Size sure can change people's views," concluded Michaelman, who also wrote an article chastising kids who vandalized bathrooms. "Your best way to express a point," he asserted, "is by ways of an underground newspaper."

But the eye did not settle on such ruminations on a cursory read of *Godhead.* What leapt out were the front-page article on Doc and the relentless return of vulgarity. Condoms and bodily fluids were back, as was scatological humor. The word *fuck* made a sensational reappearance. Fisting was mentioned prominently—and, for the uninformed, graphically defined. Mention of genitalia of both sexes abounded. Those close to Dave didn't have to guess the meaning of "Ex-lax for a certain substitute," which appeared on Gimpell's Christmas list.

As he sat in honors English first period, Dave was in his glory. They'd been controversial, all right. They'd even upstaged the *Blueprint,* which was suffering its customary production delays and wouldn't be bringing out its Christmas edition until later in the day.

All week, Drouin had been discussing the literary canon and how political correctness and multiculturalism, movements her students would encounter in college if they hadn't already, were influencing lists of "Great Books." She'd asked her students what characteristics authors of the traditional canon shared. "White," one kid said. "Men," said another. "European." "Dead!" Drouin said: "Now there is a call for greater diversity in what you read, ladies and gentlemen." Over vacation, she wanted her class to compile their own lists. In January, she would hand over her lectern so they could present them to the class, along with supportive essays. Drouin was renowned for her senior seminars—"the major event of a lifetime," she called them. Senior seminars were factored heavily into a student's average and they made many a kid sweat. But as preparation for the rigors of college, Drouin believed, they were invaluable.

At eight o'clock, Drouin was interrupted by the PA.

"Will Joel Waterman and David Bettencourt please report to the office?" the voice said.

Everyone knew what that was about.

"Told you Chief was gonna be bullshit," one kid said.

"That's it—you're suspended," said another.

Chief was behind closed doors when Joel and Dave got to the office, but his secretary, Bonnie Kistler, had a message for the boys. Organized and efficient, wife of a Baptist minister, Kistler had raised her own children according to a firm moral code. She had a sense of humor, but she found nothing funny in *Godhead 4*.

"Mr. Mitchell wants to talk to you about the newspaper," she said. "At ten-fifteen. He'd like you to bring everyone else who's responsible."

The next two hours were like the good old days: *Godhead* talk was everywhere. Many welcomed the paper's return and applauded its renewed edge, but not everyone. Seniors in the assembly were ripped that their lyrics had been stolen. Some with the in crowd thought *Godhead* had taken a shot at them again. What most infuriated some, adults especially, was this item on a *Godhead* Christmas list: "Madonna's pussy (not her cat)." Ordinarily unflappable teachers nearly went berserk when they read that. Hairy gnome scrotums were one thing, but Madonna's pussy was beyond the pale. The *Godhead*ers listened to all the talk and wondered, with increasing trepidation, what awaited them at ten-fifteen.

On the surface, Dave was unfazed. He spent part of his morning finding someone to pick up Beth, who wanted to come to the assembly—Dave couldn't sneak out for her himself because if he got caught, he'd be ineligible for tonight's game. He passed the rest of the time with Joel playing Operation Overkill, a computer game. A teacher recently had found the game in the system and banned it, but before she could erase the files, Joel had shifted them to a better hiding place.

However, Dave was worried. He'd craved controversy, but to have so many people so bullshit—it was like detonating a bomb and realizing, too late, you only needed a grenade. Well, the damage was done now. If he got suspended, there'd go basketball—no telling for how long. And there'd be hell to pay at home.

Maybe I should write a letter of apology, he thought. Maybe just kind of forget there was supposed to be a meeting.

At ten past ten, Dave and Joel went to the principal's office. For a moment, they thought they were being stood up, but then *Godhead*ers began to appear. And friends of *Godhead*ers. And kids Dave barely knew, a crowd, by ten-fifteen, of more than two dozen. Acting on the principle of safety in numbers, Gene, Ferg, and Brian Ross had actively recruited supporters all morning.

Kistler showed the boys in.

It had been a hellish morning for Chief, and not only because of *Godhead*. He had a school committee meeting to prepare for. Budget season was here. Some of his faculty were beginning to grumble about his leadership. Even in the best of times, the eve of any major holiday was crammed with business.

"Are all of you the creative editorial writers?" Chief said.

No, explained Brian; some were kids who'd only helped copy and distribute. Mitchell was skeptical that they'd had any involvement, but he didn't press the issue.

"Last time," Chief said, "I talked about respect and dignity. Respectability, if you will." He reminded the boys that he'd discussed creativity and freedom of expression—and the responsibilities that came with them.

"I did not really want to infringe on that freedom," he said. Nobody moved.

"I was not a happy camper today," Chief said. "I was very, very disturbed. I was very, very upset. This issue goes beyond the taste that I think is acceptable."

▲ *Paul Bettencourt with his oldest son.*

Chapter 9

THE ACURA

"There's a struggle going on—a power struggle."

—LESLIE BETTENCOURT

Dave didn't really believe the old Dad had disappeared. He just wasn't around as much, that's all.

The old Dad wrestled on the floor with his sons, drove them to their games, helped with their homework, took them and their sister with Mom on hikes. Paul drew up plans for Dave's tree forts and provided the materials and tools so he could build. There were no curfews to haggle over, no pointed questions about girlfriends, no pressure to get more hours at Li'l General. Chores, bedtime, and TV were sometimes battlegrounds, but the way Dave had figured, that was life. So was Dad being there when you got home from school. At the Bettencourts', Mom was the one who left for work each morning. Dad was drinking coffee and already working the phone down in his corner of the family room.

And during Dave's final year of high school, the old Dad

was there as usual after school, inquiring about his day, re-
minding him to pick up Danny or Laura, asking him to run
into Pascoag for milk or bread. Early on, Dave sought his father's counsel on *Godhead*. Paul appreciated the creativity but
was impressed more by the entrepreneurship, Dave's intuitive
understanding that it wasn't enough to publish—you had to
market your product as well. "It'll be good management practice," Paul said. "When you go to apply for a job, you can draw
back on some of the experience you had of management of
your little group here. Everything helps." Like his wife, Paul
was inquisitive the first time the *Godhead*ers came by. "Who
are these guys?" he asked his son. "Are they legit? Or are they
just going to give you a hard time?" "They're all good kids,"
Dave said.

But that Dad, Dave thought—the understanding, good-
natured Dad—was becoming scarce.

In his place was a father who seemed always on his case—
starting with that long-running number, chores. Meals, dishes,
laundry, vacuuming, grocery shopping, taking out the trash,
raking leaves, vacuuming the pool—Dave understood that
with two parents working, you were always behind. Did that
mean Dad had to hound him to death? "David, get off the
phone," Paul would say. "Take the trash out." And Dave
would answer: "Just a minute." Half an hour would pass and
he'd still be yakking. "I wasn't like that," Paul would say.
"When my father or mother said, 'I want you to do this or do
that,' I would just do it and get it over with."

But chores were no longer paramount. Paul knew someone
at the post office who knew someone at school who'd related
Dave's antics at the junior prom—the phrase "silly ass" had
been used—and now Paul kept admonishing Dave not to turn
into the crown jester of Burrillville High. He complained that
Dave never did his homework. He professed not to understand

why his son never could see enough of Beth, even when Leslie reminded him he'd been that way with her. He couldn't understand why his oldest son had no interest in power tools.

Paul's father had helped build ships during World War II, and by the time Paul was born he was a boiler fireman on the night shift at a plant in Providence. By day, he ran a company that installed home appliances. Paul was his helper. "At five years," he told Dave, "I could install a gas range." Except for tree forts, Dave had no interest in anything like that. "Hey, you want to learn some electrical?" Paul would ask. And Dave would answer: "Why do I have to know that?" And Paul would say: "Because when you have your own house and you've got to do some repairs, it's either going to cost you through the nose or you can attempt little things yourself." And his son would say: "Nah, that's OK." Paul wasn't sure Dave could change a tire. The only machines for which they shared an aptitude were computers.

A self-made man, Paul was careful with money. He considered Dave reckless.

"I can't find my wallet," Dave said one day.

"It's in the car," Leslie said.

"I told you not to leave your wallet in the car," Paul said. "People break into cars for wallets."

"In our driveway?" Dave said.

"You never know."

And Dave thought: One way or another, it always gets back to cars, doesn't it? Cars and Beth.

Dave got his license at sixteen, when he was first eligible. The first drive he wanted to take was to Boston, for a Celtics-Bulls game. Tickets weren't available, so he settled for cruising the Pascoag 500. But a license was good for more than joyriding.

A license meant Dave could play pickup basketball anywhere he wanted. He could offer car dates, prized by girls who didn't drive and would rather stay home than have some boy's parents drop you off at the movies, then pester you with questions all the way home. Dave's first car date was with Brandie Bozzi, eventually the class salutatorian, whom he took to the sophomore semiformal. In the competition for girls, a license was an incalculable advantage. For a while, it put Dave, whose birthday was early in the year, on a par with the in crowd.

A license freed the Bettencourts from chauffeur duties, but freedom came at a price. Paul and Leslie initially worried that Dave would kill himself, but as he proved himself as a motorist, their fear became a midnight call from state police. The roads were crowded with drunks, especially on weekends, and even the best defensive driver had to trust, to some extent, to fate. "It's not you we worry about," Leslie would say, "it's the other drivers on the road. You have to be very careful, very cautious." Paul and Leslie repeated this warning—and others!—often enough that Leslie began to call herself the Mother of Doom.

Dave couldn't afford his own car, and his parents, who already had three vehicles, weren't inclined to buy a fourth. The Bettencourt van was available to Dave, but it was big and boxy, not his style, nor any self-respecting girl's. Neither was Leslie's Buick, although it would do in a pinch. Dave wanted Paul's car: an Acura Integra with sunroof, cellular phone, and a sound system that could blow your head off. Paul gave his son a gas card and paid his charges. He paid the insurance and lease, which carried a penalty for exceeding a certain mileage.

"Don't put the mileage on" was all Paul asked.

"OK, Dad," Dave would say.

Then he would ignore his father, and the miles would add up, and they would argue again. When they did, Paul would always manage to slip something in about the trash.

When Leslie had Dave alone, she would say: "There's an identity thing here. You're stretching and trying to assert your right to an opinion. Dad's still trying to control. Take my car. Just take my car." Leslie even tried humor. "It's got a bigger backseat," she said, "what more do you want?" Dave wanted Dad's car. And in the end, Dad always softened. His car bans never lasted long.

The blizzard started as rain on Friday afternoon, December 11. It turned to snow that evening, as the Broncos played to their first victory of the season. By nine-thirty, when Dave left the Bronco Dome with Beth, the parking lot was deep in slush and the wind was picking up. By dawn, a foot of snow had fallen. At noon, the power went. The plows were hopelessly behind, and by nightfall Saturday, as the winds began to diminish and more than two feet of snow blanketed northwest Rhode Island, the only way to get around was on skis, snowmobile, or with four-wheel drive.

Beth had planned only to spend Friday evening at Dave's, but the driving was too treacherous to take her home. Dan was stranded at a friend's and Dave took Laura's room, freeing the boys' beds for his sister and girlfriend. Saturday was an old-fashioned New England adventure—hunkering down while Nature spent her fury. Dave, Beth, and Laura played board games and watched TV until the power failed. When it did, candles were lit, a kerosene heater fired up. Leslie cooked dinner on a camp stove. And when the family stuff wore thin, Dave and Beth retreated to his room.

Dave's notion of decorating seemed predicated on fitting as many objects into that sixteen-by-eighteen-foot space as he could: banners from fourteen sports teams, a dozen caps, plaques from youth basketball, a NO PARKING sign, a Sega Genesis 16-bit game system. His drawers held smaller treasures: a condom that his godmother, Aunt Patti, a sex-ed teacher in another town, gave him as a gag; a Red Sox ticket stub; science fair certificates from his first fair, when he was a third-grader, through his last, in junior year; a sixth-grade T-shirt proclaiming, DAVE AND SHERRY 4-EVA. He had letters from Beth and a red paper heart on which she'd written: "David Bettencourt and Bethany Sunn, July 20, 1992, till the end of time." And seventeen issues of *Sports Illustrated*, of which five were swimsuit editions, the rest Michael Jordan covers.

Dave's male friends were fixtures in his room, but Beth was the first girl to win open access. She could take or leave most of the sports stuff (some of the hats were cute), but she liked the refrigerator, the video games, and the phone, a separate line Paul and Leslie put in for their kids. After school and on weekends, Dave and Beth spent hours in his room talking, calling friends, drinking soda. They liked to make out and rough-house—the simple act of touching still excited. One afternoon, they formed letters of the alphabet with their bodies on the floor. Considering that the inner sanctum was invaded, Danny was pretty good about things . . . most of the time.

The weather cleared on Sunday. That afternoon, Beth's father made it up the Bettencourt drive in his pickup. That night, Beth wrote in her diary: "I ♥ Dave, only 1 week till our 5 month anniversary!"

It didn't take being snowbound for Leslie and Paul to realize Dave's current relationship was profoundly different than any before. Beginning with Dave's first girlfriend, they'd monitored his romantic interests as carefully as his choice of friends. They knew the standard against which Beth would be measured because they'd set it.

Stacey Rawson was Dave's first girlfriend. By senior year, she was a cheerleader with her pick of in crowd guys, but in fourth grade, when Dave became infatuated with her and she with him, she was just that sweet girl with the blond hair.

Their relationship consisted of telephone talk and a trip to the carnival, where he won a brass unicorn for her. In sixth grade, Dave began going to school dances. Two years later, he was allowed daytime dates to the mall. Girls liked Dave because he didn't come on strong. He was funny and, corny as it sounded, sensitive in a way other boys weren't—a listener, not a braggart. "Your a really good kid," one girl wrote in his eighth-grade yearbook, "your always nice to me and I appreciate that. Your never a jerk to me." He was a freshman when he first went steady; a sophomore when he first fell in love, with Libby Monfette, whom he'd met at a dance in the spring of 1991. Libby was a freshman at North Smithfield High—a pretty, smart, introspective girl who liked how Dave made her laugh. Libby didn't belong to any particular crowd. She wasn't pretentious. Except for wearing tie-dyed shirts, she wasn't into fashion statements. She liked all the Bettencourts and was happy to hang out at Dave's. "I love you, I love you, I love you!" Dave wrote to her from vacation in Florida. They lasted two months. Deciding he wasn't so funny anymore, one day Libby told Dave it was over. His reaction upset his mother, who believed good parents kept their children from needless hurt. One day, the relationship in its final moments, Leslie happened to overhear her son on the phone. He was crying.

"David, it's not worth it," she said when he hung up. "You're just too young right now to get this serious."

As they'd watched Beth that wintry weekend, the Bettencourts couldn't help but remember Dan's party. "Who's the girl in the bright yellow pants?" Paul had asked Dan.

"That's Beth Sunn," Dan said. Leslie knew Ruth, a fellow teacher.

"This can't be Ruth's daughter," Leslie said. "She looks like Madonna!"

For the first few weeks that Dave and Beth went out, the Bettencourts didn't read much into it. It wasn't as if he'd never had a girl. He didn't issue hourly bulletins on his every date and they didn't snoop—by now, they knew, trust mattered as never before. One day, Dan told Paul: "Dave and Beth are going steady, you know." Dan understood how serious they'd become. His brother would make plans to shoot hoops or play Dungeons and Dragons and then never show up, never call—guess where he was again? It was ticking the guys off, getting dissed like this. In August, Dave decided to make things official. He invited Beth home for a barbecue.

Dave's last steady relationship had been with Lauren Raspallo, the girl after Libby. Lauren was a nice girl, not given to ostentation—the kind of girl who would become the kind of woman who would marry and have a family. Beth didn't seem headed in that direction. "This is a whole different ball game," Paul said to Leslie. OK, so rap was all the rage. What about what counted? Beth didn't much like school. Some of her friends sounded questionable.

"David, you don't really need that, not with your plans," Paul said at an early juncture, when there was still hope he might sway his son. "You've got to make sure she doesn't influence you to go the other way from what you've always been taught not to do."

And Dave said: "I know what I'm doing, Dad."

Paul and Leslie weren't convinced. One of Leslie's brothers had married his high school sweetheart and only recently emerged from a divorce. Paul and Leslie had friends whose daughter, a freshman in an out-of-state college, was dating a high school boy. There was talk she wanted to transfer to a school closer to home, even drop out, in order to be with her true love.

When Dave and his parents discussed his college plans early

in his senior year, Paul said: "Apply anywhere in the country." Dave applied only to URI. You didn't need more than a second to figure that out.

Except there was another Beth, as the Bettencourts discovered the more she was around. The other Beth was not allowed TV on school nights. She had a week-night curfew of seven P.M., and Tim, in consultation with Leslie, had set midnight as the weekend curfew. The Sunns would not permit their daughter to be alone with Dave at her house or his. They insisted on knowing where she was going whenever she went out, and if plans changed, they expected her to call. Teetotalers, they demanded their daughter not drink or smoke. Beth had promised to call Tim for a ride if she ever found herself in a situation that made her uneasy in any way. If Beth really had this wild streak she sometimes projected, the Bettencourts surmised, her parents seemed serious about keeping it in control. It didn't hurt that the Sunns were taken with Dave. "Frankly," Ruth said, "I'd be content to have her marry him. I adore him. I think that he comes from a family that has values I respect."

Before long, the Bettencourts felt comfortable enough with Beth to tease her about her hair. Beth had a sense of humor. She was intelligent and, away from the crowd, surprisingly sweet. And Dave was crazy for her. When all was said and done, that was what they were up against. Their firstborn was almost eighteen.

Being that age, Dave felt no compelling need to embrace a standard of truth that would consistently pass a polygraph test, especially with regard to girls; the very nature of romantic relationships, with their possibility of physical intimacy, got in the way of that. In most regards, Dave was honest with his parents, but frankly, when Beth was involved, there were times it was to everyone's advantage to fudge things a bit.

You did not necessarily want to tell your folks the truth when you'd blown your curfew, as Dave and Beth sometimes did; one way out was saying you'd stopped by McDonald's to visit some friends on the closing shift and just sort of lost track of time. Sometimes it was best to avoid a full accounting of your day. More than once when Beth was home sick, Dave snuck out of school to hand-deliver a card or a teddy bear, but those adventures weren't always recounted at the dinner table. One day, Dave forged a note asking to be released early from school for physical therapy on his finger, which he'd injured the summer before. In reality, his appointment was with Beth.

There was a risk, though: getting nailed. Leslie was sophisticated in teenage detective work. She hardly had a choice: Between work and home, most of her life was with adolescents.

One night, a month after Dave and Beth had started going steady, they decided to go to the beach. His folks probably wouldn't mind, but why take chances? Why risk more grief about miles on the car or what they planned to do when they got there? It was easier to say they were going to the mall.

"You went to the beach," Leslie declared the next morning. She'd found sand in the car.

"No, we didn't," Dave said. "We played volleyball at Gator's Pub." Beach volleyball was big at Gator's Pub, a restaurant near Beth's house.

"David, you went to the beach," his mother said.

"No, we didn't. We went to Gator's Pub. I swear."

Then what was this Leslie had taken from the car? She held out her hand. Why, these were blades of grass! And not just any blades of grass—these were indigenous to the seashore, not the suburban lawn. With her biology background, Leslie had immediately identified them.

The funny thing was, Leslie wouldn't have minded him going to the beach. "Why do you have this need to lie," she asked, "when most of the time the answer to whatever you want to do is yes?" Dave didn't know.

"It must be a teenage thing," Leslie said.

▲ *Dave and Beth in Dave's room.*

Chapter 10

LOVE SONGS

"Girls. Jesus Christ. They can drive you crazy. They really can."

—HOLDEN CAULFIELD, IN *CATCHER IN THE RYE*

By the new year, Dave and Beth's relationship was the longest, and most intense, either had ever had. Beth trumpeted her love to family and friends, and when she couldn't be with Dave or talk to him on the phone, she wrote him letters and poems, decorated her book covers with his name, and filled her diary with her feelings for him.

"I have Dave withdrawal," she wrote one day, not twelve hours after being with him. "I need to see him a lot, and for a long time, too." She counted the days to summer, when their time together would increase.

Dave was similarly moved. "To Sun," was the name of a poem he wrote one day:

> *Yellow hair that brightens my day,*
> *"I love you and you love me," is all that I say.*

Boy, is she beautiful.
We have fun during work and play.

But alongside the poetry were less giddy emotions that spring from long-term commitment. Dave and Beth were tireless teases, and sometimes what began as ribbing degenerated, unpredictably and with frightening speed, into nasty bickering. It mattered not if they were alone, or with their parents, or among strangers at the mall. You couldn't let things slide—you had to deal with them the instant they came up! Mention of Stacey Rawson, in any context, could get Beth going, even though Stacey had a steady of her own.

But Libby and Lauren were the worst ogres from Dave's past. One day when she was in Dave's room, Beth spied his junior prom picture, which he thought he'd hidden behind the mess on his dresser. Dave had taken Lauren, and there she was with him—smiling and dressed to kill! "Why do you still have that up?" Beth demanded. "I like the picture of me," Dave said. "If you really loved me you wouldn't have it up," Beth said. "Fine! Fine! I won't keep it!" Dave said. He ripped the picture into pieces, which he later burned. It didn't help that Lauren's family ran a flower business on the oft-traveled road from Dave's to Beth's, or that Lauren's father made no secret of his belief that Dave was just the kind of guy for his daughter, or that Lauren herself during senior year had second thoughts about breaking up with Dave.

"Well, this year has been a very hard year," Lauren would write in Dave's yearbook. "I wish we would have talked a lot more this year. I still think of you as a great person and friend. I know that we didn't go out for that long, but I must say you treated me like *gold*! Thank you. I'm sorry that nothing worked out between us but at least we are 'cool' with each other . . . well, *please* keep in touch!! Love ya!! I'll miss you!

The choice is yours! Love always, Lauren." Well, Beth could fix her wagon. She wrote *her* yearbook love to Dave over a full-page ad for Lauren's family's business. "Everyone knows we'll last forever," Beth declared, "and that's all that matters."

Once, Beth passed Libby in the mall when Dave was off buying a shirt for his brother. Dave was furious when Beth mentioned who she'd seen. "I don't talk about Ryan Murphy, do I?" he said. But he did, often—cracks about what a stupid sport hockey was and how dumb hockey players were, a stereotype he didn't really believe. He teased her about Jay LaForge, who, it had lately been learned, had had a secret interest in Beth at Dan's party. And Jeff, a North Smithfield High basketball player whose cheers Beth was assigned to lead. Just to be nice, Beth made Jeff cookies one day; out of gratitude, he gave her a teddy bear.

"That you sleep with," Dave alleged.

"I don't sleep with it!" Beth said.

"Then why'd he buy you a teddy bear?" Dave said.

" 'Cause I'm his cheerleader, stupid."

Months after the drinking party, Dave had not let up on Beth. He was still afraid, obsessively so, that somehow she would come to peril. "There are guys that go to parties and look for drunk girls to take advantage of," he explained. "There was a thing in North Smithfield about points—if you got so far with a girl you got different points, and they were keeping track. That's wicked bad." It bothered Dave when he and Beth were out and a guy would look at her, especially if she were wearing an outfit that flattered her perfect figure, as she often did.

Both Dave and Beth felt a pressing need to know what the other was up to. A full report after each absence was obligatory.

"Where'd you go yesterday?" Dave said one day. He knew. They'd been over this one already.

"I went to the fucking mall," Beth said.

Dave gave her a look she knew well.

"Oh my God, David," Beth said. "Oh my God, oh my God. I feel . . . I don't know. I don't know what to say. I just don't know. You don't believe anything I fucking say."

"I didn't say that."

"Why'd you just go: 'You said you went to the mall, but whether you really did . . .' That's right, Dave."

"Well, you lied to me about other things."

"No, I didn't."

"Yeah, you told me you went to the mall with your mom," Dave said.

"I know—and then I said, 'No, I'm going with my friend Cindy.' "

"So why'd you have to say you were going with your mom?"

"Because I can't say I'm going with Cindy—'cause you'd fucking get all bent out of shape."

"Is it a guy Cindy?"

Beth couldn't believe what she was hearing. This was one of those times Dave *really* needed a grip.

"No, she's a fucking girl. OK? Cindy is a girl. And it's just too damn bad if you don't believe me."

"I believe you."

"I fucking love you, Dave. You have not said that you love me. So obviously you don't."

But he did, and after a bit he said so. They kissed and the argument was over, as quickly as it had blown up, just like their others.

There was no tidy formula governing relations between the sexes at Burrillville High. Age, maturity, weight, acne, puberty, and chance all came into play. Some kids had no interest in romance. Others experienced an aching emptiness without it. Some, not boys exclusively, thought nothing of cheating when the right opportunity came along. Certain couples broke up, made up, broke up, and made up again—country and western songs could have been written about them.

For all the walls a previous generation might have torn down, a hard truth remained: When it came to dates, looks and personality counted more than brains or sensitivity. But sexually, it was a different world than when the Bettencourts and Sunns had come of age. The seventies had seen to that. Sex, all kinds of sex—straight, gay, bisexual, kinky, group sex, cybersex, risky sex, safe sex, sex in print, on screen, and in music—sex suffused the culture.

One effect on kids was a candor unprecedented in the experience of veteran educators. Whether or not you were having sex, by senior year you almost certainly were talking openly about it. In crowd or loser, boy or girl, you weren't plugged in unless you knew (or could credibly speculate!) who was sleeping with whom, or hoped to. Most memorable escapades were on weekends, when parents were away, curfews late, and alcohol and drugs accessible. Monday-morning hall talk combined colorful rehashing with the placing of future odds: It could have been football kids were talking about. Sexual conquests impressed. Rejection was embarrassing. God forbid your failure should become common knowledge, as it did with one girl who wrote a note expressing, in terms surprisingly explicit for her, a carnal longing for a boy who couldn't have been less interested. He gave The Note, as it became known, to the *God*headers, who returned it to the girl—after they'd read it and passed it around. She was mortified! She was a romantic girl, poet not pornographer, and this had come from the soul! Now the whole school knew of her indiscretion! For the rest of the year, she lived in fear that The Note would be published in *Godhead*. But Dave was too humane for that.

Statistics show that American adolescents in the nineties are having sex earlier and with more partners, and there was no reason to believe Burrillville kids were different. Still, there were those who refrained from sex, or remained unsophisticated in its ways—the backseat of a car was no better an environment for discovering one's sexual self in the nineties than it had been in the fifties. An unscientific survey conducted by the *Blueprint* disclosed that thirty-nine seniors said they'd had sex, and ten said no; but only thirteen juniors said yes, and twenty-six no. It made for a thought-provoking juxtaposition. At the same time some kids were becoming accomplished in fellatio, others were hiding hickeys from their parents under turtlenecks and makeup.

"The pressure for sex is one of the most stressful of our high school years," Kerri Latondress, a senior, wrote in an essay for Dick Martin's class. "Your parents say they would be disappointed in you, or even forbid sex. Your religion tells you it's a sin to have sex before you're married. Your boyfriend says you would sleep with him if you really loved him. Your friends justify sex, as long as you're going out for a certain amount of time, otherwise you're easy. . . . Meanwhile, your favorite soaps, movies and music videos can make it seem as if everyone is having sex."

One of the hits on progressive radio in the 1992–93 school year was "Detachable Penis," a ballad. This was the year that raunch deejay Carolyn Fox returned to the Providence airwaves and Howard Stern arrived at Boston's WBCN, whose signal made it to Burrillville crisp and clean. Network TV played to prurience, but networks in the nineties were not the frontier. Cable TV was. In Dave's senior year, cable companies announced plans to bring Spice, Hot Choice, and the Playboy

Channel to Rhode Island's living rooms. X-rated pornography was available, for the same rental fee as *The Little Mermaid*, at the local video store. At the mall, you could buy Coed Naked T-shirts, a line with slogans such as COED NAKED BASEBALL. IF YOU'RE IN SCORING POSITION, WE'LL DRIVE YOU HOME! And just across the state line in Connecticut, the Fuzzy Grape, a strip joint, had an alcohol-free night so that eighteen- to twenty-year-olds might legally attend. For some of Burrillville's boys, the Fuzzy was a cool night out. You could come to school the next morning with a Polaroid shot of you and a woman with humongous naked breasts.

"Women are used more often than men in sexual advertising," Stacey Rawson wrote in Martin's class. Stacey singled out the purveyors of cigarettes and booze. "In these commercials," she wrote, "women are always in bathing suits. This is probably supposed to show the male that a beer will win a man a beautiful woman."

Despite feminism's gains, a double standard remained at an age when attitudes begin to gel for life. Girls who slept around were sluts, while guys were studs. Dave explained: "You can tell guys, 'If you want to have sex, have one girlfriend, and have sex with only her.' But guys aren't going to, not all of them—it's just the natural guy and girl instinct. Some guys might look for a relationship they can stay with—but why are they going to stay with the relationship?" Dave laughed. "So they can have sex later! End of story!"

If it sounded cavalier, it was not. AIDS scared many kids. Students were not shocked to learn of a pregnant classmate, but they worried it might happen to them. Drouin was reminded of how deep that fear was when three of her honors English students, two girls and a boy, chose pregnancy as their topic when writing about coming of age. Dave himself had briefly dated a girl who, many months later, became pregnant by her new boyfriend. Nonetheless, neither pregnancy nor AIDS had eliminated carelessness. Judging by the *Blueprint* survey, the condom was the most widely used contraceptive at Burrillville High, with the Pill next—but five of the eighty-eight students sampled admitted to using "nothing." One result was three unmarried seniors who gave birth, or learned they would, during the year. Another result was abortions, undocumented by any study but numbering several in the 1992–93 year, if the grapevine was to be believed.

If there were homosexuals at Burrillville High, none had come out. If someone had, the reception would have been mixed. Many seniors, including the *Godhead*ers, believed a person's sexual preference should be respected no matter what it was. Dave said: "If I found out one of my friends was gay— I don't know, it's kind of weird. If he was coming on to me and he was gay, then it'd be, like, 'See ya, wouldn't wanna be ya.' But if he was just gay and never bothered me, I wouldn't give a shit." Not all of Dave's classmates were of like mind. During a discussion of AIDS one day, a boy in his health class learned of Florida's high infection rate and said, to the teacher's reproval: "All the fags are moving to Florida. . . . We should put all these people on an island and leave them there." For kids like him, it was still acceptable to put down a loser by calling him "homo." You could still impress your friends by boasting how you'd beat the living shit out of a fag if one ever made a move on you.

The health curriculum, mandated by state law, featured handouts, charts, and videotapes of sexual topics—technical information presented in an intentionally clinical atmosphere. For a thorough exploration of the human underpinnings to re-productive biology, health class wasn't where to look. You might look to your parents, but for most kids, there was something too weird about that. If you attended church, you might look to religion—but church at seventeen was not the place to be. Those who were smart looked to teachers like Drouin.

Drouin started the new year in honors English by lecturing about female writers in English literature. To get things going, she brought in several books from her personal collection and lined them up along the board. One was a volume of horror stories by women, another an anthology of poetry by seventeenth-century women. Laughing, she put up *Inside the Male Chauvinist Mind,* a paperback whose every page was blank. The ensuing discussion of gender differences quickly developed into a brouhaha that lasted the better part of a week.

Tension first surfaced after Drouin read "Eves Apologie," a poem about the fall of Adam and Eve by Emilia Lanier, a Shakespeare contemporary. Drouin interpreted the poem as shifting blame for the fall from Eve to the serpent. What did her students think?

"It was just a bad time of the month for her," one boy said.

"Adam was weak," said a girl.

"Eve was just evil and cunning," a boy replied.

"Adam was just horny," Dave said. "It's obvious!"

"Eve was being generous in sharing the apple," Krissy Remington insisted.

"Maybe she lied," Drouin said. Drouin liked doing that sometimes—playing devil's advocate.

"Of course she did," Rob Cooper agreed. "She was a woman."

Dave said: "I think Eve should be a used-car salesman. She'd be perfect."

"She just wanted to share," said Jodie Cooke, who had feminist sensibilities. "She loved him."

Drouin wanted to know if the poem should be included in

anyone's literary canon. "Bettencourt," she said, "should it go in?"

"No."

"Why not?"

" 'Cause it's false."

But another boy wanted to include the poem. "It would give us something to laugh at," he said.

The boys applauded. The girls called them jerks.

"We women know we're better," Krissy said. "We don't even have to argue!"

In World Lit, Drouin had asked her students to list ten bad experiences they might have, then choose the worst and describe it in an essay. When they were done, she separated the class into pairs and asked everyone to read his or her partner's essay and react. "What is it that Mr. Mitchell says all the time about walking in someone else's moccasins?" Drouin said. Krissy's list included being grounded, boredom, and failure, but her worst experience was PMS. "After reading Krissy's enlightening essay," said Dave, her partner, "I can sum up how I feel in five words: Thank God I am male. She tells of how often men ask: What's the matter with you—you must be on the rag. I had no idea why Beth chases me with a meat cleaver when I ask that! Now I know that this really upsets women. I shall never do this again."

Several weeks later, in mid-March, when winter refused to leave and spirits were flagging, Drouin sought to energize World Lit. "Ladies and gentlemen," she announced, "time for a new theme. In the next fifteen minutes, you will write the history of men and women. Probably the first fifteen-minute history of men and women ever written!" When time was up, she asked for volunteers. Several boys' hands shot up.

"Do we wish to make note that those who aggressively sought to be first were all men?" she joked.

Scott Bridge's history was a fable set at the dawn of time. Drouin loved it. Another boy's history began then, too, but its premise, that women had emerged from the sea as "slime," offended Drouin, even though she chose to believe he'd intended humor. "In order to appreciate slime, you have to be slime first," she said, with a rare bite to her voice. Krissy argued that in creating men and women, God had struck a balance. Marcy Coleman's history was based on the premise that women, "the ultimate human," had been created smarter, more rational, and "more in touch with their emotions than their male counterparts," although she would have excepted Justin Laferrier, last fall's Mister Bronco, whom she had recently started dating. Marcy's conclusion made the class erupt again: "If men say that they are superior and women are inferior, then why do men trust women to mother their children, nurse the sick, and teach the young in schools?"

Dave's history aimed at laughs, but he slipped in a truth at the end:

> After Adam and Eve, God figured he would try different things. He tried to create a whole group of women on earth, but this failed because they were unable to work without men. Then, God tried a large group of men. They worked fine together, living like slobs, eating TV dinners, and watching football games. However, God knew they could use some help with the cooking and cleaning. Blam! Women. Now, men and women could work in harmony. They would work fine for millions of years and women would eventually even become close to equal to men.
>
> So, women can't live without men and men have a hard time without women. Let's leave it at that.

Pregnancy, birth, nursing—Dave was familiar with the particulars of reproduction. There were two younger siblings in the house and his aunts were having children, and no one hid anything. As puberty neared, the Bettencourts gave their son a book about sex and said they were there for any questions. He barely asked any. That was fine with Paul, but it disappointed Leslie, who taught biology and had once taught sex ed. "You never have this moment where you sit and have this major discussion," she lamented. Still, her offer to talk remained open as Dave started dating. Sometimes when her son was going out for the evening, she would make a crack about carrying a condom. A light touch, she believed, would give Dave entree if ever there was something he wanted to discuss. There almost never was.

Sometimes, as Beth left the Sunns' with Dave, Ruth would ask what they were going to do between nine-thirty, when the mall closed, and midnight curfew. "We're going to have sex, Ma," Beth would joke. Ruth didn't believe it, but not because the Sunns had shied from the topic with their daughter. They'd talked about pregnancy and disease and advised how to defend against attempted rape: "Kick him in the balls and run like hell" were Tim's instructions. They insisted that sex belonged as part of a commitment between people in love, but not people in love at her age. "You're too young emotionally, too young physically," Ruth would say. "We want you to wait. You'll understand when you get older that it's not good for you to experiment." And Beth would reply: "Oh, Ma, a lot of people don't do it—they just brag about it."

Dave and Beth thought about all they'd been told, discussed it, and came to a decision. And what it was, they would tell you, was not for the world, or even their friends, to know.

▲ *Brian Ross, Superfan.*

Chapter 11

HELLHOUND

"I try to be positive, even about negative things."

—MICHAEL JORDAN

When basketball began, it looked to be another season in hockey's shadow. The Bronco Dome would half fill, mostly friends and relatives of players, and a small cheerleading squad. The game would be played. Marcotte would phone in the results to the papers, the janitor would shut off the lights, and that would be that.

But the first contest, held on a Tuesday night, drew almost a full house—including a sizable in-crowd contingent, a promising sign. The second game, Matt Stone, Pete Godfrin, and Jason Cleary, hockey tri-captains, dropped by after their practice to lend support. As December went by and the basketball team did OK, but no better, attendance climbed.

Something was going on. You couldn't ascribe it to winter—true, cold weather gave kids cabin fever, but basketball in Burrillville had never been the cure. Perhaps hockey was responsible: This was a rebuilding year, which meant basketball might be more exciting by default. Maybe it was some spillover effect from the NBA, which had Michael Jordan and Shaquille O'Neal, pitchmen for a marketing machine so effective not even small towns could escape the sell. Maybe it was Wignot's players. When it came to guts, no team in recent memory could match these Broncos. They were underdogs with heart, and that had powerful appeal.

Or perhaps it was the phenomenon that came to be known as the Superfans—a collection of kids, primarily *Godhead*ers, whose antics were as offbeat as the Bronco Dome's design.

Most of the kids who turned into Superfans were at the Broncos' home opener, but their behavior was not aberrant in any way, except perhaps the special attention to their favorite player, the illustrious Venison Chef, Terry Gimpell. A week later, Joel and Matt Leveille arrived at the Bronco Dome with a golf club and a red pole. Tied to Joel's club was a tattered white shirt on which he'd spray-painted "BHS." Matt's banner was an old pillowcase. On time-outs, when they made madcap dashes around the court, the crowd was delirious. Encouraged, the Superfans added new members and expanded their act, until, by the end of December, kids were as enthusiastic for them as they were for the Broncos.

By January, Superfandom was complete. Matt and Joel carried their trademark banners and Matt wore green trousers, a coonskin cap, and a checkered sports jacket with a label identifying it as Made in Japan. Gene and Tebow blew plastic horns. Cote kept a toothbrush behind his ear—"because you should brush after every meal," he explained. Michaelman carried plastic jugs of milk—"for inspiration," he told a policeman after an away game. ("Did it work?" the cop asked. "Yeah," Michaelman said. "I'm sorry," a girl who'd been listening said as she walked away, "but youse people are too weird for me.")

Jay LaForge had the most creative taunts, Brian Ross the most creative costume: white lab coat, mismatched sneakers, panty hose and red goggles on his head, a look indebted to Frank Zappa and *Seinfeld*'s Kramer. The only one not outlandish in some way was Joel's new girlfriend, Tracy Auclair, a quiet, dark-haired freshman who wrote poetry and inspired Joel to do the same.

If the Superfans had a leader, Brian was it. Brian's parents divorced after he was born and he was raised by his mother and stepfather. He had one of the strongest work ethics of anyone at Burrillville High, holding a year-round job at Village IGA and, summers, a second job at the day camp where Beth worked. Brian loved the Beatles, Bob Dylan, Nirvana, and the Who, and his music collection included more than twelve hundred albums. He played guitar very well and sang not as well, and he'd been in six rock bands, including one called 8 Million Horseshoe Head and another called Cerebral Pastry. He loved to laugh and what delighted him was shocking people, especially adults. Being a Superfan gave him unprecedented opportunity.

During breaks in games, he would run the circumference of the gym, turn, and charge down the middle of the court. Sometimes, Joel would meet him and they would collide— chest to chest, like slam dancers. Other times, Brian would continue downcourt toward the cinderblock wall. He won't do it, those who'd never seen him would think, but he would. He'd leap headfirst into the wall, crumple to the floor, twitch as if dying, then jump to his feet and run back up into the stands, always to tremendous student applause. Some adults, his mother included, were amused. Some were clueless: Was he some sort of bizarre cheerleader? Someone's demented cousin? Others were offended, and they were the ones that tickled Brian most.

"I wonder if he feels it," one disgusted middle-aged man re-marked at an away game.

"Yeah, I felt it—and it felt good!" Brian responded.

With the two losses that followed the Broncos' defeat in Bar-rington, Wignot tried just about everything. He changed of-fense, stepped up the pace of practices, dissected games they'd won and games they'd lost. He shuffled starters and substi-tutes. The season was nearing the halfway point and it had been proven, painfully, that the Broncos would never leave the cellar on talent alone.

As depressing as things had become, Wignot never yelled. He never criticized without also complimenting—sandwich-ing, he called it, wrapping disapproval in praise. He remained on the lookout for kids who had problems at home, and as much as he wanted to win, there were times he kept someone in a game even when his play was awful because he knew benching him could have repercussions in areas that transcended sports. Wignot had the ability to coach in college, and he had the con-nections, through Providence College's summer camp, where he'd been on staff. But the college game, with its recruiting and pressure to win, wasn't for him. High school was.

"You've got this little society that lives together for three months out of the year," he said, "and they have to put up with the good, the bad, the ugly, and everything else that goes on. You learn a lot out of that—how to get along with people, that some people are going to be the shooters and some people are going to be the rebounders. Just like in society."

Wignot believed public schools had become too permissive, and in making his case, he cited the language and clothing stu-dents in the nineties are allowed. "I think kids aren't made to be responsible for a lot of their actions anymore," he said. "We find excuses for why they do everything they do."

In the arena where he had some control, he was conservative. He did not let cheerleaders sit with players on the team bus. He wanted his players well dressed. He did not like foul language or rude behavior at games.

By mid-January, he was regularly witnessing both.

When they couldn't be on the court, the Superfans performed from the stands. Some nights they were so loud that Matt got headaches and he and his friends left games hoarse. "Goin' home in a body bag!" LaForge yelled at opposing players; "Take your Ritalin!" at a hyperactive coach. To break the concentration of opponents at the foul line, Superfans led the chant: "Bull-shit! Bull-shit!" They were merciless with referees. One short fellow with dark hair and a mustache endured a night of being called Mario, the video-game character he resembled. An overweight ref was repeatedly advised to seek the services of Jenny Craig.

It was debatable whether the Superfans incited others to rowdyism. Whatever the reason, Burrillville fans had a growing reputation around Rhode Island as boorish and crude. Home or away, Bronco boosters did not hesitate to call an opponent "butt-reamer." One boy named Cinquegrana became "gonorrhea." "I had your mother!" a Bronco backer shouted at another opponent. ("No, you didn't!" the mother shouted back!) Most Burrillville fans weren't rude, of course, and not all the coarseness came from kids. One of the foulest mouths belonged to a Bronco father. "Take the whistle out of your ass and blow it the right way!" he shouted at refs.

"Dear Mr. Mitchell, I am writing this letter in anger," Wignot typed into his computer late one night in January. "It's the anger and embarrassment I've had to bring home especially after our last four games."

Wignot described the Superfans as a gang and complained

that during an away game, they'd barreled through the host team's cheerleaders during their halftime show. He described how humiliating it was always apologizing to referees and opposing coaches, especially in light of his having won two statewide sportsmanship awards (voted by the referees' association) in recent years. He linked fan behavior to changes in school, and society at large. "It begins with the little things like wearing hats in school," he wrote. "It festers with the breakdown of the dress code, allowing students to wear shorts, T-shirts, and the like to classes. . . ."

On the morning of January 15, the day the Broncos were to play at North Smithfield, Chief got on the PA. He told the students about Wignot's concerns and he said bad behavior would not be tolerated at the Bronco Dome or anywhere else Burrillville played. He did not specify what sanctions awaited violators, but he warned they would be harsh; once again, the bottom line was respect.

After his address, Chief summoned Brian to his office. Wignot had advised closing the bleachers behind the Broncos, but Chief wasn't going that far yet: He hoped restraining the head Superfan would suffice. Henceforth, he said, Brian was confined to standing immediately in front of the Burrillville bleachers. He was specifically forbidden to slam Joel or leap into walls.

It was not a popular position with players or fans. Finally, basketball was cool, and what does the administration do? Put them down! No one denied the language had gotten out of hand, but did that mean they had to crush the Superfans? What about hockey? There were fights all the time at hockey games —on and off the ice!—what did they ever do about *that*? "Why are they so fucking anal?" Matt said at lunch, where Chief's dictum was the only topic. One Superfan thought they should just ignore their principal. Another thought they should up the ante: lighting a fire in a trash barrel during a game, then

extinguishing it with their urine would be an appropriate statement, he submitted. But Superfans already were on shaky
ground on account of *Godhead 4,* and the eventual consensus
was that they should seek a second chance.

Later in the day, Gene, Joel, and Brian went back to Chief.
It was unfair, they argued, to place all the blame on them.
What could they do about a hot-tempered father or kids who
came to games drunk? Besides, the Broncos really appreciated
their Superfans—just ask Dave Bettencourt. Compared with
last year, when the team went 6–11 and nobody had cared,
Superfans had helped make every game this season seem like
March Madness! Wasn't everyone always saying how important school spirit was? If they promised to behave, could they
have one more chance, please? Chief relented. Just to be sure,
he decided he or Doc would attend all home games, and as
many away as they could.

"There is in each life a moment of crisis," Drouin said in
World Lit one day the week after the loss to Barrington. "Has
anyone had a moment of crisis? I think we've all had lots of
moments of crisis."

For a week, her topic had been Dante's *Inferno,* the journey
of a man through hell. It begins in dark woods, where Dante
meets three beasts. "If you had to identify a beast," Drouin
said, "something that gets in your path—external or internal,
something big or something small—what would it be? And
how would you get around it?" When her students were done
writing, Dawes had created the Wizard of Wickedness, Krissy
Remington the Serpent of Stubbornness, Michelle Bynum the
Werewolf of Worry. One kid—the boy who had compared
women to slime—claimed to have no beast. No one bought
that. "A man with no beast lies to himself," Scott Bridge said.

Marcy Coleman wrote of the Eagle of Eternal Control.

Marcy's father was a kitchen designer; her mother, a teacher at the Providence Hebrew Day School. Her mother had her best interests in mind, but lately, it seemed, didn't approve of anything Marcy did. She didn't think Marcy was pushing hard enough in school, even though she was ranked first and in no danger of being displaced. She didn't like Justin Laferrier, whom Marcy had been dating. She didn't like the career Marcy was considering: chemical engineering. Mrs. Coleman wanted Marcy to pursue premed.

"I don't want to be a doctor," Marcy said.

"You'd make me so happy," Mrs. Coleman said.

"But what about *me*?" Marcy said. "What about what makes me happy?"

In her essay, Marcy planned to have a talk with the Eagle of External Control. "I hope that maybe she will understand and remember how she felt when she was a baby trying to leave the nest," Marcy wrote. "However, if this doesn't work, I could always tie her wings together when she is sleeping and toss her out of the nest. I think a three-hundred-foot drop would solve the problem quickly."

Dave's beast was the Hellhound of Humor. He volunteered to read his essay to the class.

"When I go overboard with my humor," he began, "the hellhound pops up and is a definite barrier. This hellhound might get me in trouble with authoritative figures.

"The way to get by this vile beast is to use my humor carefully. I should use my humor for good only, not be forced to the dark side. If I bring my funny side too far, some of the acts that I am involved in may look immature and childish. This is something I do not want, since I do not want to have a certain reputation. However, if humor is used properly, I can win."

Drouin thanked Dave for his essay. "Moderation in all things," she said, "including in moderation! That's good.

Being truly humorous is a gift. But if you're a funny person, you have to stay in control."

Drouin was privately thrilled. In December, she'd heard about his shenanigans, but she felt professionally restricted from talking to him, at least then, because whatever was happening wasn't on her watch. She hoped the Christmas break would be a catalyst for change—she'd seen vacation have that effect before. If it didn't, she'd vowed to have a talk, she and Ronald Brissette, who also had his eye on Dave.

"I care about you and I think you're wonderful and tremendous," Drouin had decided to say, "but if this continues, it's going to affect the way that I feel about you. And if that doesn't matter to you, I guess that's OK. But I think it does."

What Drouin did not know was that for the first time in his life, Dave had been tormented.

Over the holidays, he'd kept thinking about the shitstorm over *Godhead 4* and the day he'd been kicked out of class. He was still mad at Mindy Ryan—but about the yearbook deadlines he'd blown, he had to admit she was right. Basketball reminded him of how he missed his grandfather. He'd dedicated his final season to Papa, but it would end shortly and still he hadn't started. In a month, he'd be eighteen, and while his life wouldn't instantly change, he understood this birthday would be different than any other, that becoming a legal adult was the beginning of a road that eventually brought big responsibilities. Even Christmas had not been without complication. He gave Beth Play-Doh, *Sesame Street* coloring books, and a stuffed Big Bird, among other gifts, and she gave him a silk tie, an Ice Cube tape, and a Sacramento Kings cap, among others—and that was all very cool. Christmas Eve was cool—until they visited one of Beth's relatives. When Beth was out of the room, he looked Dave in the eye and said: "You break her heart, and I'll shoot you with my gun!" Dave didn't know if he was kidding or drunk or what, but it was unsettling.

On his walks through the Round Top woods—on days when dusk came by four o'clock, darkness before five—he felt burdened as never before. Things sure could get complicated, couldn't they? He didn't tell anyone, but on several nights he couldn't sleep. The last time he'd had insomnia this bad was after watching *Poltergeist* when he was a little kid. He found inspiration in his grandfather, a diabetic who, before he died, had an infection that led to gangrene.

"He needed to get his lower leg amputated," Dave wrote in another World Lit essay, "but this did not stop him. He continued to work. He continued to love his family. He didn't let this ailment stop him. I, today, continue on when pressed into a corner. Things may be going bad, but I will not give up. That was important to him and it's important to me."

The insomnia passed, but not the misery on the court. "We need a win, big-time," Dave declared after the Broncos' third consecutive loss, on January 12.

It came the very next game, when the Broncos beat North Smithfield. The Northmen were no powerhouse, but for the sake of morale, any win was blessed. The season was half over, and the Broncos until tonight were 3–8.

"Feel a little better today?" Wignot said after the game.

"Of course!" several players said.

"Let's go guys, build off this," said Dave, who recapped the evening in his diary: "Yay! Yipee! We finally won another game. We beat North Smithfield 56–34. It was extra good because it was in my girlfriend's hometown. It was extra, extra good because I started my first varsity game. Beth cheered very

nicely. I must say she does look good in that cheering outfit."
("Well, my advisor said that if I cheer for Dave she will pull me
off the bench," Beth wrote in her diary. "I cheered for the
Dave on our team but I was really cheering for my Dave! Shh,
don't tell anyone.")

Wignot's decision to start Dave, at point guard, was not
courtesy. There was a danger in this in-your-face style of ball
he was trying to get the Broncos to play: You could overdo it,
and what was intended to intimidate could become five boys
running in circles, easy prey for a well-coordinated attack.
"You can be too haphazard at it," Wignot said, and what he
wanted beneath the chaos was a foundation of order. Dave's
strength was his brain; already, he was coaching youth-league
basketball and consistently winning. Wignot considered that a
good sign, but what persuaded him was how Dave brought intelligence to his own play. Under pressure, Dave remained
cool. He had an instinctive sense of how to pace and when to
regroup. "He thinks basketball rather than just plays it," Wignot said.

But the glow from North Smithfield faded the very next
game, a loss at home to Bristol. Wignot couldn't forget the
near-comeback against Barrington. He'd seen that intensity in
other games and he was convinced that attitude was the key—
that when the Broncos believed they could do it, they did it.
With Dave starting, he was pretty sure he had his lineup for
the rest of the year. All the team needed now was a jolt.

The day after the Bristol loss, Wignot announced that from
now on, players wouldn't receive their uniforms until immediately before a game—if they were to receive them at all. Forget
about whether you were starting—you might be watching from
the stands! Nobody was safe! Everybody's ass was on the line!

"This comes as a major shock," Dave said. "I hope it
works."

It didn't. The next game was a loss, one that opened with Scituate scoring fifteen unanswered points, the most dismal seven and a half minutes of a season that had become unbearably long.

So nobody was in a good mood four days later when the Broncos boarded the bus for the half-hour ride to Central Falls, a city on the Blackstone River. Prosperous during Rhode Island's textiles era, it was now the state's poorest community, a place so hungry for economic revival that it lobbied, successfully, to be the home of a jail. The state ran its school system, and nearly three quarters of its students ate free or reduced-price lunches. The annual dropout rate was more than 18 percent, four times the state average.

Central Falls was known for drugs and violence, not without reason. Immigration of law-abiding Colombians had been accompanied by the arrival of a small but enterprising criminal element, and by the 1980s, when even *Rolling Stone* magazine wrote about it, the city was notorious in law-enforcement circles as a distribution center for cocaine coming into New England. People got shot in Central Falls, sometimes over drugs, sometimes in gang warfare, and sometimes by tragic coincidence. In a case that did not enhance the city's reputation, two buses carrying a visiting basketball team from a middle-class community not unlike Burrillville were attacked in 1990 by rock-throwing kids. For two years, Wignot and other suburban coaches refused to take their teams into the city.

Not surprisingly, the Broncos were not paying tribute to Central Falls when their bus pulled up to the high school. Nobody missed the chains on the entrance to the gym, or the cop, or the fact that the door to the men's room was intentionally kept open. Everybody knew why they were playing at five-thirty P.M., two hours earlier than any other game. If they needed further proof they weren't in Burrillville, they found it in flyers posted on the locker-room bulletin board. One announced meetings of a support group for gay and lesbian adolescents, another the start of "a multicultural AIDS education program for teens." Before leaving the locker room, Wignot advised his players to bring their valuables with them to the bench, where they could be watched at all times.

"We've got to get some wins under our belt," Wignot said as they took the floor. "The playoffs are approaching."

Burrillville scored first and never trailed in the first quarter but was behind by seven at the half, by fourteen two minutes into the third. Here we go again, Wignot thought—down the toilet! And then it happened—the Barrington syndrome again, a bolt of confidence from somewhere, the Broncos getting their doors blown off one minute, and the next transforming themselves into basketball superheroes. By the end of the third, Burrillville had a one-point lead. "This is a hell of a comeback," Wignot said to Marcotte. And it lasted, as Burrillville won 70–64. Dave turned in a fabulous game, playing with poise and scoring seven points, his season high.

"About time, boys!" Kevin Blanchette said. "About fucking time!"

"That's a legitimate team," Wignot said. "You didn't beat a North Smithfield. We've got to keep going at that pace until we get to the civic center floor!"

There were no fights at Central Falls, no drug deals, guns, knives, vandalized buses, or off-color cheers. The crowd was enthusiastic and big, a rainbow. In the faces of some of the kids, you saw the Emerald Isle; in others, the Orient; still others, Central or South America or the Caribbean. If the ghosts of Central Falls' mills symbolized America's past, the home crowd at the high school was a peek into its future.

The Broncos left Central Falls without trouble. The trouble began on the ride home, when Jay, one of the instigators of the food fight, started needling Kevin Blanchette. Jay was a nice kid, but he had a temper. Wignot liked him, thought him decent at heart, and he was willing to overlook off-court behavior—fights, mostly—he wouldn't have tolerated on a team. Jay played soccer for Wignot, as well as basketball. "Wait till you get this kid," people used to say to Wignot, "he'll never make it a year with you." To which Wignot had replied: "Well, we'll see what he does." What he'd done was become an outstanding player in both sports and made progress toward controlling his temper, another reminder to Wignot of why he coached kids.

Wignot was at the front of the bus and didn't see what was transpiring down back. It wasn't what he would have ordered up to celebrate the win that just might have saved the season, but it wasn't a surprise. Wignot had detected tension recently between Kev and Jay. Maybe it was that Kev was playing most of every game, while Jay was mostly on the bench. Maybe Jay didn't like the way he thought Kev had looked at his girl, a gorgeous cheerleader who was on the verge of breaking up with him. As the Broncos left the city, Jay started teasing Kev about *his* girl—specifically, her teeth—by singing the tune to *Mister Ed.*

Kev finally had his fill. If Jay wanted to fight, he'd be waiting when they got back to Burrillville High. As they were getting off the bus, Jay punched Kev. Teammates quickly got between them and no one was hurt, but now Wignot had a problem.

This wasn't just anyone Jay had taken a shot at. This was Kev—tall, lean, graceful Kev, a kid with a dry sense of humor who called friends "homeboys" and carried a beeper so they could keep in touch. Kev dressed hip, kept his hair short, and wore an earring, which he took out before practices and games—a confident but not cocky kid who handled his celebrity the way Matt Stone and Krissy Remington handled theirs. Kev, Dave, Dawes, and Bridge had grown up shooting hoops together, but only Kev had a legitimate chance at playing college ball. He was the team MVP—the franchise, such as it was.

Wignot was torn. You got places standing by kids—just look at Jeff Fague. Junior year, Jeff had been suspended for fights, and few believed he'd turn himself around. Wignot had taken a chance on him, and he was paying his coach back this year with good behavior, on and off the court. But Jay had gone too far, in front of the entire team. To let him off with only mild discipline—what kind of message would that send his teammates? Wignot thought about it overnight and decided he had no choice. After writing up a report, he and Doc told Jay he was off the team. "It's a failure for me," Wignot said, but he would not change his mind.

After Central Falls, it kept happening—the chemistry, the confidence, whatever it was. In their next game, the Broncos beat Scituate by twenty-one. The game after that, they beat a traditionally tough Ponaganset—at Ponaganset. By the end of February, the Broncos had a regular-season record of 10–9 and were in the playoffs, facing Barrington in the first round.

This time, Barrington was coming to the Bronco Dome.

▲ *Dave at his surprise eighteenth-birthday party.*
Gene, Jay Cote, and Dave's brother, Dan, are behind
him.

Chapter 12

WINDMILLS

"I'm 18. Wow! I never thought I'd get here."

—FROM THE DIARY OF DAVE BETTENCOURT

Dave often replayed that scene in the principal's office the morning of the Christmas assembly—how he and more than two dozen boys, all allegedly *Godhead*ers, had stood there while Chief told them how badly they'd let him down. He'd trusted them to keep *Godhead* clean, and what had they produced? Smut.

"I'm embarrassed, totally embarrassed," Chief said. "That's immaturity. I find it offensive. I find it in very poor taste."

He was referring to the line about Madonna's private parts, which Madonna herself was publicizing in her bestselling book of photographs, *Sex*. Chief said *Godhead 4* gave him reason to rant, but he was curbing that impulse. "I don't know how effective that would be," he said. "I'm trying to get to your heads." It was a never-ending problem at Burrillville High: getting to kids' heads.

Chief laid it all out again: language, judgment, taste. What students thought or said privately, he said, was their business. But *Total Godhead,* with circulation schoolwide and beyond, was public.

"What will the community say?" Chief said.

No one answered.

"Try to stick to your community's standards."

Bruce Walls asked if it was ever acceptable to use the word *fuck.* He defined community as the school, where, along with stronger stuff, *fuck* was an everyday word.

"The question is," Chief said, "is the message you're trying to convey enhanced with the use of that word?" Not in the principal's view.

Chief urged the *Godhead*ers to conduct a serious critique of their paper, "a post-production analysis," he called it. Like Paul Bettencourt, he suggested they find a way to maintain impact without being so offensive.

"Gentlemen, you're growing," Chief said. "You're also growing intellectually. I'm not going to make any further judgments at this point. Put all those beautiful attributes the good Lord has given you to good use. I'll judge you by the next one that comes out."

Dave promised to take today's lessons to heart. "When we graduate," he said, "we want to give it to the juniors, sophomores, and freshmen."

Chief dismissed the boys on a note of levity. "It's a good thing I like deer meat," he said, in reference to the *Godhead* article about Doc. The boys laughed.

"Happy holidays, gentlemen."

The boys tumbled out of Chief's office. "A *Godhead* victory!" Dave proclaimed, but he was playing to the boys. Not only did Dave want to bequeath *Godhead* to underclassmen— what an awesome tradition to start!—he wanted to put out another issue or two before he graduated. He hadn't forgotten what Dick Martin had said about the reputation he'd leave behind. He didn't want to be remembered as a punk.

Shortly before the assembly, Dave, dressed as Marcia Brady, stood with the rest of the senior cast in the Bronco Dome as Polacek scolded the *Godhead*ers. They'd done more than steal lyrics, he said; they'd violated a trust. Was this the thanks he got for giving up so many evenings to the class of '93? In order to proceed with the assembly, Polacek said he was putting the controversy aside, for now; he would deal with the snitch or snitches when he found out who they were . . . and by the way, he would find out. If they'd been thinking about starring in the senior play, they'd better think again.

Despite *Godhead*'s transgression, the assembly, including the not-so-secret song, drew the usual great applause. Everyone cheered cafeteria supervisor Florence Champagne, who was observing twenty-five years at Burrillville High, an anniversary that probably would have passed uncelebrated had Dave not informed Polacek when the assembly was being planned.

When it was over, Dave went to Chief, alone, and confessed that he'd been quietly uncomfortable with *Godhead 4*. "I think the way to go now," he said, "is back to our old humor. No vulgarity." Dave promised Chief the next issue would be clean. Somewhat later, he gave his father his word, too. Paul had finally seen *Godhead 4*—Dan's copy, not one of Dave's!—and after reading it, he'd talked to his oldest son. "David," he'd said, "if you're not going to let me read them before you do them, then you've got to use more common sense and judgment, and don't allow this to happen again."

Dave was not himself that second week of February. It was like the time around New Year's, when he'd had insomnia—except now, his birthday had him blue. Sunday was the big day, and about the only thing anybody had said was that there would be a joint celebration for him and his cousin, who was turning two.

"Everyone loves 2 year olds," Dave told his diary. "18 year olds are just kinda there. I guess I got to get used to it. . . . Everyone thinks I'm always happy-go-lucky. For the most part I am, but this week I'm just waaah. Oh, well." The only one who seemed to care was Drouin. On Friday, the last day of school before winter recess, she led her honors English class in singing "Happy Birthday" for Dave and Joel, who turned eighteen right after his friend.

Now it was Friday night and the weather was lousy, a plague of sleet and snow that made the roads too hazardous to go to the mall. Dave's game had been canceled. Two days until his birthday, and still no one had said much about it.

"No one remembers," he said.

"It'll be OK," Beth said.

"I'm going to be an adult and I'm going to graduate and I don't even have a party anymore 'cause my dad thinks I'm too old."

Dave was driving. He'd picked Beth up at home and now they were heading through the storm to Dave's house, to watch *Indiana Jones and the Last Crusade*. Beth had never seen it but Dave had, at least three or four times.

"Aren't your relatives going to have a party?" Beth said.

"Yeah—for my two-year-old cousin. Maybe they'll, like, throw my name into the song or something."

"You'll get lots of money and gifts and stuff."

"Right."

Dave turned onto his road, past Round Top fishing area. He couldn't see the cars parked around the bend.

"Maybe I'll invite my close friends over for a party," Dave said. Maybe co-host something with Joel.

They went inside and Dave went upstairs for the videotape.

The living room and kitchen were dark. He almost ran into his parents in the hall.

"Where are you going?" Leslie said.

"I'm getting *Indiana Jones.*"

"Do you, ah, want some orange juice?"

"Ma, leave me alone."

"The movie's in the kitchen," Paul said.

"OK," Dave said.

When he got to the kitchen, the lights came on. His sister, Laura, had baked a cake. The living room was decorated with Batman balloons, Batman paper plates, and Batman party favors. Basketball players and most of the *Godhead*ers, a dozen kids in all, burst from hiding.

"Surprise!" they shouted. No one could remember the last time Dave had been speechless.

He was a legal adult now. He was entitled to gamble and he did, the next week, winning one dollar on Keno, a state-operated video game. He could sign his own permission slips for field trips and he could vote, although with no election soon, he didn't register immediately. He exchanged his juvenile license for an adult one. He was supposed to register for the draft but didn't bother until after receiving a warning in the mail. Lured by free M&Ms and Coke, he applied for a J. C. Penney charge card at the mall. With his father as cosigner, he opened his first checking account and received his first ATM card. He put it in his wallet next to his Batman card, which said: "As an honorary *Batman Returns* member, the bearer of this card vows to preserve the peace, uphold justice and stand for truth."

It didn't feel like he was a real grown-up. Real grown-ups had gray hair, flabby middles, and serious demeanors, and their brains seemed different than kids'. Take computers: Why was it that so many grown-ups were clueless when the biggest sped kid on earth could figure out a new program in about fifteen seconds? Why couldn't most people over thirty grasp that Dungeons and Dragons was a game without an end? "No one wins, Ma!"—how many times had he said *that*? And what was this with the face-lifts? Why did so many middle-aged people, and not only movie stars, have their faces cut? Their *faces*—it hurt to say it! "Half their lives over anyway," Dave said. "I can see maybe if they got half their face burned and needed it, but just to do it because you want to look better—it's dumb."

What bothered Dave more than anything was that adults (most, anyway) seemed to have less fun, and he vowed that wouldn't be him. "I don't want to wear my pants up to my neck and talk about the government all the time!" he said. He imagined living to a ripe old age—ninety-five sounded about right—and never losing his sense of humor. When the end came, it would be serene, just like the final scene in some sentimental movie. He would be on his deathbed, surrounded by his family, and he would say good-bye to them one by one. When it was his great-grandson's turn, Papa would wish him luck in his next game. Dave's great-grandson, his namesake, was going to be a star in the NBA. Dave was certain of it.

Chief believed in second chances. Depending on the circumstances, he was sometimes good for a third or a fourth. When he'd been in high school, hadn't his principal done the same for him? Didn't he owe some of his success to educators who knew what went on inside the mind of a boy?

But the practical reality was that the *Godhead*ers weren't operating in an ivory tower. Chief answered to a superintendent who was upset that *Godhead* not only hadn't gone away, but seemed in some perverse way to be thriving. Chief had a coach who'd written a letter that could be read as an indictment of his leadership on the issue dearest to him, respect. Teachers who'd been divided over *Godhead* supported restrictions now, while those who'd disliked it from the start figured they had what they needed to kill it. At the January faculty meeting, a music teacher esteemed by her peers said *Godhead* should be put on next month's agenda. Word was she would settle for nothing less than an absolute ban.

"They can't do that," Dave said. "But it's awesome teachers are talking about us! It means we're noticed."

In late January, Chief told Dave what Dave already knew: *Godhead* was in serious jeopardy.

"Don't worry," Dave said. "The next one's going to be a clean political satire."

But it was too late: Mitchell already had asked the school department's lawyer to outline options. On February 9, Dave was summoned to the office. Dave's right to publish was constitutionally protected, Chief said, but the school was within its rights to prohibit distribution on school grounds, and as of today, *Godhead* was banned. The next day, Dave and Michaelman pleaded for another chance, without success. The *Godhead*ers felt betrayed: Hadn't Chief given them one more chance? Then again, hadn't they promised to clean up their act before *Godhead 4*? Maybe that was life.

In any event, they weren't about to roll over now.

We'll hand it out on the street, they vowed. Mail it to kids at home! Or change the name—it was *Godhead* that was banned, wasn't it? Maybe they'd find a school that didn't have an underground newspaper and start one there! Blame it on someone else—that junior wannabe would be perfect! Perhaps they could parody the *Blueprint*, writing funny stories and calling it the *Spewprint*. Or fashion themselves after the *National Enquirer* and put out an issue of off-the-wall pieces. What

most appealed to Dave was political humor. PARLIAMENT DIS-
SOLVED: QUEEN TAKES CONTROL OF ENGLAND! is one of the
headlines he imagined. BRITS IN U.S. ASSASSINATE CLINTON
AND DECLARE U.S. A MONARCHY!

But weeks passed and *Godhead* was comatose. Once in a
while someone asked what was going on, and if you looked
carefully, you could still find Andre the Giant stickers on ceilings and walls. A kid who was clueless about fashion wrote a
letter to Terry Gimpell explaining, in his way, why different
cliques dressed the way they did. ("I don't fit in to any group
in this school," he concluded. "If I do, I don't know it.") And
in Martin's class, Rob Eddy completed a Valentine's Day assignment on metaphors by writing this: "Love is like *Total
Godhead,* you say something wrong and you're up the creek."
But that was the extent of it. Even D. B. Lover hadn't been
heard from since the last round of letters, back in the fall.

In an "exclusive" interview published in the St. Patrick's
Day issue of the *Blueprint,* Terry Gimpell explained: "We
made a mistake and it ruined our newspaper. I think it was
well-liked by the students. Our mistake was a big letdown to
others and we lost respect. We'll be back."

But all that appeared was a flyer Dave and Joel left on wind-
shields during the hockey team's post-season dance. The flyer
reprinted the First Amendment, which guarantees a free press,
and a passage from the *San Francisco Oracle,* an alternative
newspaper in the seventies. Dave had come across it doing research for a History Day project he and some *Godhead*ers were
putting together on the underground press:

"Who is the Underground? You are, if you think, dream,
work and build towards the improvements and changes in
your life, your social and personal environments, towards the
expectations of a better existence.

"Courtesy of *Total Godhead,*" the flyer was signed.

—

When Drouin heard all the commotion over *Godhead 4,* she declined to read it. If it were as bad as its reputation, she knew her relationship with Dave would be tainted and she would not be able to defend it publicly. Besides, she had more pressing matters. Her honors English students were ready for their senior seminars.

"OK, seminarians," Drouin said after instructing her students to arrange their desks in a circle. Dave's name had been drawn to go first.

"David, are you ready?"

"Yes."

"Ladies and gentlemen, David Bettencourt!"

After light applause, Dave began reading his essay. His delivery was smooth, his tone scholarly. He stumbled only once, on the word *coincidence.*

"While the traditional canon has all men," he concluded, "my canon would consist of men and women of all race and nationality. Different types of literature, such as plays, novels, short stories and poems add a nice touch to the canon. Also, horror, fiction, non-fiction, and autobiographies make for an interesting canon that has a lot of literary firepower." Dave's canon had works by Shakespeare, Tolkien, Dickinson, Dickens, Irish poet Eavan Boland, Mary Shelley, and Salman Rushdie. He included Mark Twain's *The Adventures of Huckleberry Finn* and Alex Haley's *The Autobiography of Malcom X.*

Next, Dave read a favorite poem, as Drouin had requested everyone to do. It was Robert Frost's "The Road Not Taken," which, he told the class, he first read at his grandfather's summer house.

"Later, I made this decision in life," Dave said. "I often took the road less traveled, because I wanted to be myself. And that has made all the difference." He received a standing ovation.

"Very interesting," Drouin said.

The final part of senior seminar was fielding a question from a fellow student. TammyLyn Dupuis had Dave. "Which book out of your canon best supports your position and why?" she said.

"I think all of them do."

"Answer the question!" Drouin said.

"I thought I did."

"David . . ."

Dave thought a moment and said: "I think *The Autobiography of Malcolm X*," a work, he explained, that best embodied the diversity missing from the traditional canon. Dave had not read every word of Haley's monumental work, but he'd seen *X* when it came out.

"That was a good choice, David," Drouin said. "That was wonderful."

After a flurry of exams and last-minute papers, second semester began. Before moving on to Cervantes, Drouin, tired and nursing a cold, allowed herself one slow day in World Lit. It was the dead of winter, a day TammyLyn wished for a woodstove. Drouin loved that idea, and imagining its warmth brought to mind a fantasy—that one morning she would answer her door and Ed McMahon would be there to hand over a $10 million check from the Publishers Clearinghouse sweepstakes!

"What would you do with it?" someone asked.

Open a school, of course, Drouin said. The Drouin Academy would be a special place, exclusively for students such as hers now. A school with real scientists conducting research, and an English class, taught by her, that would periodically cross the Atlantic on "literary discovery trips" to England and

Ireland, home of her ancestors. The students were off. They'd go to her school! They'd even help build it! They'd have visiting artists, resident writers, a recording studio, a theater, and courses on horror writing and film.

"Oh, it would be wonderful!" Drouin said. "I could hire you to be seniors forever! Can you imagine it?"

The discussion flowed naturally into Cervantes. Drouin asked everyone to list five personal impossible dreams, in order of impossibility. "Put yourself in Don Quixote's place," she said. "What would your windmills be?"

Kelly O'Rourke wanted to be a cartoon character, or a snowflake falling to the ground. Krissy Remington wanted an end to suffering and pain. Beth Stone wanted to find out what heaven was really like, Marcy Coleman to be a fly on the wall when Lizzie Borden took her ax to her parents. Dawes wanted universal respect, regardless of race, sexual orientation, or dress. "If you have an earring you're queer—you know, that mentality," he said. Dave's impossible dreams included living in the Middle Ages, everlasting youth, becoming a character in Dungeons and Dragons, and, like Han Solo, fighting the Empire in outer space. And he wanted to play professional basketball.

The hype on Monday, February 22, was incredible at Burrillville High. Everybody was talking about tonight. The Superfans had posted signs everywhere. A *Godhead*er had slipped a bulletin into the pile of morning announcements, and it was read over the PA: "This evening at seven-thirty the boys' basketball team will host Barrington High in the first round of the play-off tournament," the notice said. "This will be the team's first home play-off game in three years. Plan to attend and lend your support. *T.G.*"

It was a wicked rush, but by the end of the day, Dave was

overwhelmed by it. For the first time he could remember, his stomach was queasy because of a game. The Bronco Dome was sold out! The newspapers would be there! All his relatives! Beth! There would be no more chances after tonight, no three-out-of-five or four-out-of-seven, like in the pros. A loss would end the season.

After school, Dave sought solace in the woods. Alone, he walked out onto Round Top pond until the ice cracked and he was afraid he'd fall in. Back on shore, he let his mind wander. It went where it usually did, to a safe place, fantasy—to Terry Brooks, a favorite author.

Calmer, he picked up Beth at five. They went to McDonald's. Dave ordered his customary three burgers but couldn't finish them, although he managed a few of the chocolate-chip cookies Beth had baked. He was at the Bronco Dome by 5:45, and as Superfans put up more signs he shot hoops with Beth until it was time to dress. "They're going to win. They have to win!" said Beth, who was wearing the ring Dave had given her for Valentine's Day.

Sleet was falling as the Barrington Eagles pulled into Burrillville High. Looking at them, you knew this was latrine duty. Could you be any farther to nowhere than Burrillville? Did every house have a chainsaw? Or maybe a 12-gauge? And check out this domed gym they'd heard about! It really did look like the mother ship in *Close Encounters of the Third Kind*!

Dave kissed Beth and ran downstairs to dress. Wignot went over some pointers about the trap and the press and then said: "Keep the pressure on. Don't get yourself out of it mentally. It's no different than any other game. It's on our court, it's to our advantage. Any questions?" There were none.

"Let's do it!" Kevin Blanchette said.

The crowd was what Dave had expected: standing-room only; Brian Ross with an electric guitar and amp; nine Bronco cheerleaders, more than in any other game; the in crowd; the hockey team; Superfans, hyper as never before. Even Drouin, clueless when it came to sports, had come.

"Welcome to the Terrordome!" Jay LaForge shouted when the Eagles came running out. "I am your worst nightmare!"

The Broncos were down by seven at the half, but Wignot didn't sound worried. "This is where we've been winning games—in the third quarter," he said in the locker room. "We're in good shape."

But after three, the Broncos trailed by five. "This is where the mental part of it comes in," Wignot said before the fourth quarter. "Keep your heads in it."

With 4:43 left in the game, Burrillville was behind by ten. Wignot called a time-out.

"For you seniors, this is it," he said. "It could be your final four minutes. It's all up to you."

A minute and a half passed without a basket. Then Burrillville scored. And scored again, and again until, with forty-seven seconds left, it was a one-point game. The crowd, which had fallen silent, was out of control again. Dave was somewhere else, in Chicago or Boston or L.A., some arena where his basketball hero took to the air while a national TV audience watched, spellbound.

It's like this for Michael Jordan, isn't it? Dave thought. This feeling that nothing can stop us now!

Barrington has the ball.

Barrington drives downcourt—and fouls—fouls Kev! The best shooter on the team is at the line!

He hits his first! The game is tied at 56!

He hits his second! The Broncos are up by one!

With sixteen seconds left, Barrington scores. Four seconds later, Armstrong is fouled. Armstrong—not the best shooter on the team—at the line.

He hits them both!

Barrington is desperate. They start downcourt.

Bridge is fouled! The Eagles are falling apart! Bridge hits twice and the Eagles are heading home with a 61–58 loss! Broncomania rules!

In the locker room, Wignot congratulated his team. Ahead was the second round of play-offs, which would be watched by thousands at a college gym. Ahead was a week of hard practice.

"Savor the moment, guys," Wignot said, "and then tomorrow, forget about it."

Was he kidding? Forget about the greatest game of their lives? No way! Dave got a copy of the game tape. He'd only scored once, a pretty layup in the first quarter, but all week he replayed that one basket over and over.

"Holy shit!" he wrote in his diary. "That was the most unbelievable game I have ever witnessed, never mind played in. I've seen tons of memorable NBA games, but I never thought I would be involved in a similar game. It was truly awesome. The feeling after the buzzer was amazing. Fans going wild, my parents (even Dad) hugging me, kissing Beth—it was all so wonderful! I wish I could just go over that moment over and over again. . . . If only it could last forever."

Reality returned two days later, when Kev went down in practice with an ankle injury. There goes the season, Dave thought—we'll never win without Kev.

"Everybody's just got to put a little more effort in," Wignot said, but it was hardly encouraging that by week's end, Kev could barely walk. And while everyone got a boost watching him suit up before taking the court at the Community College of Rhode Island that Saturday night, nobody missed him soaking his ankle in a bucket the team manager had filled with snow.

On paper, Burrillville seemed no match for its second-round opponent: Bristol, Class C-Two regular-season champs. As the preceding game neared its end, Wignot sketched out the plan. The strategy was nothing new: relentless pressure at both ends of the court. "Other than that," Wignot said, "it's just a matter of when you get this far into the playoffs, if you really want it, you've got to believe."

Burrillville scored first, Dave next, for a 4–0 lead, but a few minutes later, the Broncos trailed 12–6. At the half, they were tied at 23. The Broncos trailed throughout most of the third quarter, but with 4:19 left in the fourth, they fought back. Colin Brady put Burrillville ahead with a foul shot.

"This is totally nerve-wracking," said Leslie, who'd sent her son off to the game with a note that said: "Best of luck, Dave, you'll be the Killer B." ("Corny," Dave said.)

The Superfans were insane. "Come on, ref, we get better calls with MCI!" "Wanna borrow my contacts?" But their enthusiasm evaporated when Bristol went on an eight-point run.

"That's it," Leslie said.

"Real tough now," said Paul.

Kev had played most of the game. He'd scored only ten points, half an ordinary night's work, but just having him there helped psyche the Broncos. When he fouled out, with 1:07 left and Burrillville behind by five, everyone knew how the night would end. Dave's foul with less than a minute to go was devastating.

"This sucks," said Jay LaForge.

"I hate this," Leslie said.

"It's all over! It's all over!" the Bristol fans began to chant, and they were right: Bristol won by ten. For the seniors, the civic center would forever be a dream.

In the locker room, Dave was close to tears.

"No complaints," Wignot said. "I don't think any of you can say you didn't go out there and play as hard as you can play . . . a few bad bounces toward the end . . . those are the breaks of the game. That's the way it is in life and that's the way it is in basketball. You can't say you didn't have a great season. You overachieved what people thought you should have done. . . .

"OK. Make sure we get those uniforms back on the hangers so I can wash them one last time."

Spring

▲ *Dave and brother Dan wrestle in their room.*

Chapter 13

LORD OF THE FLIES

"Who are you fighting against?"

—DAVID KORESH

Had there ever been a more violent year than 1993? Dave wondered. Only April, and look what had happened already. Religious fanatics had almost taken down the World Trade Center with a bomb. Police officers were going on trial again in the Rodney King case, and the evening news was filled with replays of his beating and the one trucker Reginald Denny got when the riots began. In Waco, Texas, the government siege of the Branch Davidians had ended in a firestorm that took the lives of more than eighty children, women, and men. The maiming and killing in Bosnia and Herzegovina went on and on.

And yet all that wasn't what brought death home to Dave like never before. It was events that took place in a four-day period within a forty-five-mile radius of Burrillville.

Five teenagers and a school nurse met violent ends April 12

to April 15, spring vacation week for Burrillville High. The first was a freshman who was stabbed in front of classmates at Dartmouth High School; three sixteen-year-olds were charged. Two days later in Acushnet (like Dartmouth, a small town in Massachusetts near Rhode Island), a deranged man walked into a middle school and unloaded a shotgun into the school nurse, who'd returned to work only that morning after cancer surgery. The next morning, three teens, including two from Burrillville, were shot execution-style in rural Foster, population 4,074, two towns south of Burrillville. That night, an adolescent stabbed an eighteen-year-old to death in Westerly, a resort on the Rhode Island coast.

Steve Mitchell was out of town when he heard. Before coming to Burrillville, he'd been assistant principal at Ponaganset High, which serves Foster, and he understood how the killings would affect the town. He didn't know the victims—the two Burrillville kids were not at Burrillville High—but he knew the alleged assailant, a Foster cop who'd graduated from Ponaganset in 1987, as quiet and polite. The fact that he was a cop was what really unhinged Chief, who believed there was no higher calling than law enforcement. This was not only tragedy—this was sacrilege, the ultimate disrespect.

When Chief returned from vacation, another of his students who'd become a cop dropped by his house. "Be careful this week," the officer warned, "because there can be copycat types of fallout as a result of this." Chief agreed. "We don't bury our heads in the sand and say it can't happen here," he said. His first thought was Minority Street Posse. Word had it that some MSP members had carried guns and knives during the tension with the hockey team the previous year, and while none had ever surfaced at school, one boy had been charged with illegal possession of a firearm when police found an unloaded .22-caliber pistol—a Saturday night special—in his car.

When classes resumed on Monday, April 19, the morning announcer led students in the Pledge of Allegiance and then Chief got on to ask everyone to remember those killed the week before. "Our thoughts are with the families of these individuals. And if you will join me now for a moment of silence." Students bowed their heads. Judging the risk of copycat killings to be low, Chief did not take such measures as metal detectors or police on the premises. His precautions were deliberately subtle. Locally, there had been some fistfights over vacation, including one in which brass knuckles had been used and another involving a boy who'd earlier punched out a girl for cutting in the lunch line, and Chief paid close attention to the participants back at Burrillville High. He ordered all but the front doors locked and he made sure he, Doc, and the staff were more visible around school. But the only weapons they saw were the *Godhead*ers' Super Soakers, back from winter storage.

As Dave watched the news, he was troubled.

Wasn't anywhere safe anymore? Look at all those mass murders at McDonald's, of all places! At postal workers who went mental with assault rifles! Hospitals should still be safe, but they weren't: Just last December, a woman had been sentenced to twelve years in prison for snatching a newborn from Providence's Women & Infants Hospital, where Dave had been born. By now, with pedophile priests no stranger to the front page, you knew the Catholic Church wasn't safe—but if you needed a hometown reminder, you got it the week after the Foster shootings, when a Burrillville man joined six others in bringing a sexual-assault suit against a priest who'd been assistant pastor in the 1970s at a church in Pascoag. Even parties could be deadly: Look at the young man who'd been murdered in North Smithfield over the Thanksgiving holiday by alleged killers no older than Dave. And no one forgot six years ago, when the so-called Blackstone Valley Snipers wounded four people in a series of after-dark rifle attacks on homes that made the governor so jittery he called out the National Guard. It turned out the two snipers had attended Burrillville High.

Dave couldn't get it, no matter how he tried. OK, so he and the guys and even Beth walked around with water pistols and cap guns—but none of them had the urge to pack a real weapon. Dave had fired real guns once—a pistol and an M-1 rifle at his father's club—but he'd never asked to go back. *Godhead* had violence, but that was make-believe. That was words on a page. D. B. Lover had threatened Beth, but nothing had come of it, that was words on a page, too. Dave still felt safe at Burrillville High, but he couldn't help but wonder.

"It should just be over girlfriends and stuff," he said, "that's what it used to be. You know— 'You stole my girlfriend, so let's fight at the bus ramp.' We fight, we get suspended from school, when we come back you don't talk to me and I don't talk to you and it's over with.

"Now it's: 'I'll take my gun and shoot you while you're walking down the street.' "

"Do you realize what last week was?" Drouin said when honors English resumed on Monday, April 19. "Your last little spring vacation!"

She paused, Chief's commemoration fresh in her mind.

"It was one of those unsafe and unsound weeks," she continued. "That's all right. I'll take care of you."

The next morning, not twenty-four hours after federal agents stormed David Koresh's compound, Drouin's topic happened to be *Lord of the Flies,* the novel about boys stranded on an island—paradise, at first. Before vacation, Drouin had asked her students to describe their personal paradise. Dave had written: "The setting would be a small, uninhabited tropical island with a big lagoon. An old abandoned McDonald's, fully operational with tons of food, rests near the abandoned Taco Bell. A basketball court is in the middle of the jungle. As for people, only Beth and I would live on the island, but I could fly in my friends anytime I want."

Before moving forward with *Lord of the Flies,* Drouin gave her kids the opportunity to discuss Waco. There was as much black humor as concern, and after stifling the jokes, Drouin said: "I suppose in a way Koresh thought he was creating a spiritual paradise. Very, very interesting. What do you have to say? Basic nature of man—evil? No? Yes?"

In the ensuing debate, divisions developed. Fourteen students believed mankind was basically evil, ten basically good, and three maintained humans are born blank slates.

"The root of man is not evil," Dave volunteered, "but evil can be switched on like a light switch when it is needed. How else can you explain how calm, rational men will kill for their country in long, bloody wars? Some have the ability to turn the evil side off, some do not. Some are just evil through and through, like Jeffrey Dahmer."

"What did you say at the beginning—it's there in everybody?" Drouin said.

"Yeah," Dave said—probably, he figured, even in him. He remembered a Fourth of July when he was twelve or thirteen, how he'd caught a frog and tried to send it for a ride on a bottle rocket—how when that didn't work, he'd pulverized it with firecrackers. ("It was cool, but it got boring after a while.") And what about his pumpkin-smashing days, the signs he'd stolen, the day this spring he and Joel had stolen a hubcap off Rob Cooper's car? None of that was truly evil . . . but it wasn't exactly what you'd call morally upright, either. And it was of his own free will. He'd had to choose between right and wrong.

"You can turn it on and off," Drouin said.

"Right. Some people, it never comes up. Some other people, it's always there, like Dahmer."

"That's a really good character to choose, a really good example. And then on the other side of that—is there an opposite to Dahmer?"

Yes, Dave said. "Gandhi or something like that."

A week later, Drouin was showing *Lord of the Flies,* the film. Students groaned watching Piggy killed by a rock, but most were morbidly fascinated, in a way they hadn't been reading the book. Joel was out of the room for Piggy's death scene, and when he returned, Dave went to the VCR and replayed it.

"David, you're a bad boy," Drouin said.

"Again!" Joel cried.

"David, don't you do Piggy again."

But he did.

In her senior lecture a month later, one of the girls whose first-semester essays had been inspired by *Faces of Death* again made violence her topic. She showed clips from two movies: *King Lear* (the scene in which the Earl of Gloucester's eyes are plucked out) and *Silence of the Lambs* (in which Hannibal Lector eats a guard's face). "This is an awesome movie!" Dave said. "I hope you all have a wonderful lunch today," said Drouin, who admitted even she had seen *Silence,* albeit with her eyes covered during many scenes.

"As a whole, society seems to enjoy watching horrible, bloody murders, people inflicting pain upon others for fun, as well as trashy love stories," the girl said in her lecture. "Are we the first generation of people to demand these assets in a good movie or book? I think not."

To prove violence's innate appeal, she asked her classmates how they would react if they came upon a hallway fight.

"Do you like to see someone's nose broke," she said, "or would you rather see the individuals walk away from each other? How about when you're driving down the road and a plow slams into an oncoming car. Don't you want to see what happened?"

Wherever you came down in the nature-nurture debate, there was no question in Drouin's mind that even late in childhood, kids bound for a lifetime of trouble could be saved. Drouin knew because over the years, she'd had more than one kid like Jeff Fague.

Jeff was no bigger than average, but he was strong and quick, and even unperturbed he had the aura of a street fighter. You didn't tangle with Jeff unless you lacked for brains or had something to prove, as someone always seemed to. Because it wasn't only aura with Jeff. Something would set him off— often, it involved girls—and he would literally go blind with rage, punching and kick-boxing with moves he'd seen in ninja movies. When finally it flamed out, somebody was bleeding or crumpled on the floor. "I don't think" is how he described his rage. "All I see is what I'm doing. That's it. I don't see windows, I don't see grass, the floor. Everything's black."

And yet there was an underlying goodness in Jeff, a paradoxical sweetness and vulnerability, something Drouin, Chief, and Wignot—and girls, who were attracted to his darkly handsome looks—picked up on.

Jeff's father, Richard, was an Irish-American from Woonsocket; his mother, Mary Jane Garcia, a Mexican-American from Brackettville, Texas, twenty miles east of the Rio Grande. Richard had had his own troubles—at fifteen, he'd been thrown out of Burrillville High for grabbing the principal by the throat. He wanted to make it as a country and western singer, and as he pursued his dream, taking whatever work there was to keep food on the family table, the Fagues were on the move: Burrillville, Kentucky, Connecticut, and Texas, where he'd met Mary Jane. Jeff was in fourth grade in Brackettville when a white bully called him a spic; Jeff broke his jaw with one punch. Jeff was paddled by his teacher, but the boy didn't mess with him again. There was no more trouble until eighth grade, when Jeff and his parents, brother, and sister were living in Connecticut. Jeff got into several fights that year, with boys who came at him first. He found respect playing football, basketball, and baseball.

By 1990, the Fagues were back in Burrillville. Jeff's sophomore year was uneventful, but by eleventh grade, he was with a crowd that was stealing radar detectors and car radios. There was cash in it, but the main motivation was thrills. Jeff was a founding member of MSP, an ethnically mixed group of boys (a Cape Verdean, three whites, an African-American, and a Hispanic, Jeff) who started as an amateur dance act, but whom the all-white cops considered bad news. In July 1992, Jeff and two other boys were arrested for breaking into a house and taking two guns and eight hundred dollars in cash. Awaiting an appearance in court, he spent a weekend at the state training school.

"I don't want to go back," he vowed. "I want to straighten my life out, get it all back on line."

The road back is not easy, not when the cops know your name. But Jeff's family was behind him. He had friends, among them Justin Laferrier, who'd been working, successfully, on controlling a temper of his own. Justin had spent the first part of high school goofing off, but by senior year knew if he didn't soon change, time would run out. On a whim, he auditioned for a part in a school play and discovered a flair for acting. He was headed for the marines after graduation, and then to Northeastern University, where he planned to pursue psychology and drama. Justin was a listener with a knack for framing problems in ways that suggested solutions, as Marcy Coleman had found out seeking advice about her mom. He believed in new starts. Like Wignot, he believed team sports build character, and so it was fortuitous that he played football with Jeff their last year in high school.

Of all Jeff's boosters, none was more influential than Drouin. She'd been his English teacher junior year, and except for his parents, coach, and principal, she was the only adult who'd kept faith. "Calm down," she'd say when she found him ready to go off. "You're not going to get anywhere if you lose your cool." Between crises, they sat for hours and talked.

"You won't have a future for yourself if you keep up like this," Drouin would say. "I don't want that to happen to you. There's too much good." Jeff didn't have Drouin senior year, but she made time for him anyway. Her letter of recommendation helped sway a family court judge to give Jeff a suspended sentence, rather than send him back to the training school. Drouin was not only a teacher: She was a Partington, a name that was sterling in Rhode Island. Her uncle was the Providence police commissioner and her father had been a captain in the state police.

By spring, Jeff planned to attend community college and become—a policeman! Before graduating, he was moved to write Drouin a poem. It ended:

I'll leave school with a lesson that you taught me
not English, or Shakespeare, but of who I was about to be.
You told me something about the power of the mind
and you were right, to make it, I just had to be kind.

Early in the spring, the subject in honors English was *Catcher in the Rye,* a novel whose hero, Holden Caulfield, has a tortuous coming of age.

"What does that mean," she said, "coming of age? Who will define it for me? Have I come of age?"

Several students said yes, she had. Born in 1954 in Cumberland, the Blackstone Valley town where she still lived, Drouin was raised with music and books. Words were magical, the doorway to faraway places and times. At Cumberland High School, Drouin fought for the abolition of the dress code and was one of the students who defended the school paper when it published an unflattering piece about a local politician. She'd loved singing since early childhood, and Pendragon, her band, satisfied her need for music. Teaching kept her where she most wanted to be: in the company of young minds.

"Is there a bittersweet quality to coming of age?" she asked. "What is it that you have to leave behind?"

"Youth," Dave said.

"Hair," said another student.

"Teeth."

"Health."

"The happiness of childhood," Drouin said. "Think about it this way: Do you remember a point in recent years when Christmas wasn't quite the same?"

"Yeah," said Dave, "when instead of toys you get fruitcake!"

Jeffrey Lesperance remembered a snowstorm over the winter. "We went sledding," he said, "and the hills were good, they were OK, but they weren't awesome. They weren't as big. They'd shrunk."

"I remember every night kissing my mom and dad goodnight and saying, 'See you in the morning,' " said Stacey Rawson.

"I remember when my dad would come home and we'd run to the door and give him a kiss and a hug," said Tiara Dimond.

Krissy Remington remembered when her father used to give

her horsey rides. "Now," said Missy Beauchamp, her best friend, "he'd be dead!"

In late March, Matt Stone had become a hero. The hockey team had surpassed preseason expectations, making it to the Met B division championship series, a best-of-three contest. Burrillville took the first game; Cranston, the regular season ti-tlist, the second. The teams were deadlocked at the end of the third. Matt had the flu, and if he hadn't argued with coach Mike Menard to play—hadn't convinced him of the terrible importance of suiting up for his last high school game!—he wouldn't have been on the ice. But he was, and it was his goal twenty-seven seconds into sudden-death overtime that gave the Broncos another state crown. His picture was in the paper, and Burrillville Midgets and Sprites all knew his name.

The very next day, he had to clean out his locker at Levy Rink, which was closing until fall.

"That wasn't too fun," Matt said. "And an alumni game— I'll have to play against high school kids."

"Coming of age should be fun," Drouin said, "but some-times it's not."

Dave described how unbelievable he'd felt during the final minutes of the Barrington play-off game. "You just looked up in the stands when we were down by ten," he told the class, "at all the parents—they weren't doing anything! It was the last time we would see that crowd!—and then we tied it! Then when we went up! I was ecstatic!"

"But even you, Bettencourt, aren't entirely happy," said Drouin.

"Uh-huh."

Impossible, Drouin said. "It's human nature."

Dave knew it was true. No matter what else happened in

life, he would never make it to the civic center. "I am very disappointed and heartbroken," he wrote in his diary immediately after the loss to Bristol.

But time was bringing perspective.

"Man, life has been boring without basketball," he wrote several days later. "I miss the practices, the games, the hype, the sweat, the basketball-smelling hands. But I'll live. I've got plenty of things to do—D and D, Beth, pickup B-ball, etc. It definitely won't be boring."

▲ *Drouin and Chief at the Literary Arts Festival.*

Chapter 14

CEREBRAL PASTRY

"Look out, Spielberg!"

—DAVE BETTENCOURT

Robins returned and lawns turned green. Baseball and tennis practices began. Senioritis hit and no one was immune, not even honors kids. "I'm sick of school," Dave said. One day, he slipped away to McDonald's, where he picked up breakfast for Beth, who'd stayed home from school. Another time, he and Beth bunked class to visit the zoo in Providence. "We saw polar bears, snakes, seals, elephants, antelope, elk, and two monkeys having sex," Dave told his diary. "What a day!"

On the second Wednesday of May, Krissy Remington went to Drouin's blackboard, erased three numbers, and wrote three more. Since March, Krissy had been keeping the countdown. It now read:

> *13 days to exams.*
> *20 days of school until graduation.*
> *30 days counting weekends and exams.*

"In four days," Matt Stone said, "we're in single digits."

"Don't do that!" Drouin said.

But like them, she was powerless; on some mornings, you could smell summer in the air. The day before had been that kind of day. The temperature had set a record, 93 degrees, and carloads of kids had made the year's first pilgrimage to the beach. Many were walking around school looking like they'd spent the day inside a nuclear reactor, but that was cool.

Looking back, time seemed to have gone into a warp: One day Mom was reading you bedtime stories, and the next you were planning your senior prom. Seniors were overcome with nostalgia, bittersweet like nothing before. Memories cropped up constantly: of favorite grammar school teachers, songs from sixth grade, old boyfriends and girlfriends, classmates who'd dropped out along the way, events as recent as last fall's Spirit Week. You couldn't get through lunch without someone saying something that set the whole table off. In-crowd kids suddenly had time for losers—*losers!* Seniors who'd barely spoken throughout high school now found themselves in animated conversation, a phenomenon they referred to as "coming together." A few were eager to leave it all behind, but for most, the past seemed safer than what was ahead.

May exhausted Drouin. She was done with college recommendations, but scholarship applications were due and, as usual, she'd been asked to write dozens of letters. If only that damn computer worked, she might have been OK. The new Pendragon album was out and critics were pestering her for interviews. Her daughter was about to graduate from Cumberland High. She was behind schedule on senior lectures. Most tiring was last-minute work on the Literary Arts Festival, as sure a sign as lilacs that graduation was near. The festival was May 20, and for the first time, Pendragon would perform at it. Tired as she was, Drouin was excited.

Drouin had many reasons for founding the festival, now in its seventh year, but prime was her desire to open minds, and not just students'. Thanks to friendships and favors, Drouin had been able to bring a rich selection of creative talents to Burrillville High at a very low cost. Rock musicians with national followings had played at her festival, as had reggae bands, Scottish harpists, and Irish fiddlers. Dance companies had performed, poets read. Comedians and filmmakers had come. This year's program included folklorists, an illustrator of children's books, the artistic director of a professional theater company, a Blackstone Valley historian, and a *Total Godhead* workshop, organized by Dave.

"If it were up to me," Drouin said in a yearbook article, "there would be a Literary Arts Festival every year, and the measure of what we know and have learned would be demonstrated in the stories we would write and tell, the plays we would perform, the reading and books we would share, and the words that would dance across the pages."

The festival opened with BHS Unplugged—performances by Ferg's band, Desolation, and Cerebral Pastry, which was Brian Ross, Justin Michaelman, and Jon Brooks, Dave's basketball teammate. There had been some minor controversy over Cerebral Pastry—was the name intended to ridicule the disabled? No way, the guys insisted, it was just two cool-sounding words that popped into Gene's head one day at Kmart! In the introduction she wrote for Chief to read, Drouin emphasized it signified food for the head, or some such. Cerebral Pastry got its biggest applause playing the theme to *Cheers,* whose final episode was airing that night. The class of '93 had chosen it for their graduation song.

Cerebral Pastry cleared the stage, and it was almost time for awards. But first, Drouin had given Justin Laferrier permission to read a poem. Like Jeff Fague, Justin's success senior year had given him perspective on how close he'd been to failure. Other seniors had realized too late, among them a girl who wanted to be a movie star. She'd appeared on the amateur stage, to some acclaim, but her passion for acting hadn't spilled over into study. She was consistently late with assignments and always hitting on someone for their homework or notes. She had a boyfriend who lived near Boston, and often she extended her weekend through Monday to stay with him. Sometimes, she just stayed home in bed. Until second semester, it did not seem to occur to her that past a certain point, her diploma would be imperiled, the college she hoped to attend out of the question. For this senior, it would be too late. She would not have the credits to graduate.

Justin said his poem was especially for underclassmen, who still had time.

"So heed these words my friends and be sure not to forget," he read, "there is nothing so empty as a heart that's been filled with regret."

Dave searched and searched for a way to publish *Godhead 5* without pissing everyone off.

Finally, he had it! He would wrap *Godhead* into the protective mantle of the Literary Arts Festival. What a fiendish stroke—Papa, the politician, would have been proud! In April, Dave and the *Godhead*ers had presented a paper on the history of the underground press at History Day, held at Brown University, and the presentation had been well received, though it was no prizewinner. For Literary Arts, he'd take the scholarly approach: freedom of the press, constitutional rights—Mom, apple pie, and the American Way! Marketed like this, Dave figured, Drouin had to be receptive.

She was, after Dave gave his solemn promise that everything

would be aboveboard. She had a suggestion on how Dave could further legitimize the workshop: invite a professional to speak. Her choice was Rudy Cheeks, a radio talk-show host who had long written for the alternative press, most recently as a columnist for *The Providence Phoenix,* a weekly with roots in the sixties. Drouin respected Cheeks, whose *Phoenix* column tweaked politicians and power brokers. Drouin knew better than to be heavy-handed with her principal, and on the agenda she submitted for his approval, "Total Phoenixhead—Alternative Press Workshop" appeared as an afterthought at the bottom of the last page. Chief signed the agenda without a word.

In advance of the festival, Dave papered the school with flyers and had this message in the personals section of the May 14 *Blueprint:* "From Terry Gimpell, in Hawaii. Aloha! It's really nice in Honolulu. I'll be back at BHS on May 20 during Literary Arts. Go to my workshop, you will love me." Two *Godhead* workshops were held. Both were packed. With her parents' permission, Beth bunked school to come and Jay LaForge snuck in. Cheeks gave a brief history of the underground press and complimented Dave and the boys for their pluck.

"You're in a long and notorious tradition," Cheeks said. "It's a good release and people need that."

Dave explained how to stuff a *Godhead* into a locker without getting caught, and he and the boys disclosed *Godhead*'s origins in last summer's yearbook meeting. Mindy Ryan took a picture. Dave passed out a list of twenty questions students could ask—"Total Questionhead . . . Look like a genius!"— and when the formal remarks were concluded, kids asked a few. When it was over, they left with copies of *Godhead 5* and orders to distribute them throughout the school. Drouin joked about how ironic it would be if, like Jan Wenner, publisher of *Rolling Stone,* Dave parlayed his publication into national success. Who knew? Ferg was headed to URI with Dave, and already they were talking of jointly publishing *Godhead* in Kingston. *Godhead*ers planning to attend Rhode Island College were considering launching an edition there. And Cote was promising a shipboard column from the navy. "When you're rich and famous," Drouin said, "will you give us jobs?" Any job she wanted, Dave said.

"So did you miss us?" Terry Gimpell asked in the lead article of *Godhead 5.* "I'm sure the school committee didn't." He couldn't resist a poke. But Dave had been true to his word; this *Godhead* was clean. Two pages long, it included an obituary for wrestler Andre the Giant, unofficial *Godhead* mascot, who'd died since issue four; a diatribe against smoking in the bathrooms; a whack at politicians; jokes ("Why is there braille at drive-up bank ATM machines?"); and an ad for the next episode of *Oprah:* "Barbie's Gay Myth."

> No more swearing, no more verbal attacks on anyone, and no more mentioning of famous people's anatomy, just comic relief in a school that definitely needs it. In a world of violence and corruption, for once we hope people can hold hands and sing after they read this issue of *T.G.* Kiss someone you ordinarily wouldn't kiss. Hug that English teacher of yours. Go out and dance in the tulips. Make the world a better place. But most of all, enjoy your reading of *Total Godhead.* Thank you.

A power outage hit Burrillville High the Tuesday before senior prom. Dave and the *Godhead*ers were in the *Blueprint* office when the lights flickered and the computers crashed.

"Power's out," Dave shouted. "We're all going to die!"

"L.A.! Riot!"

"Let's steal yearbooks!"

"Yeah!" Dave said. As punishment for Senior Bunk Day, when dozens of kids had skipped school on the Friday after Literary Arts, Chief had postponed release of the '93 *Review.* The books were still in cartons in Ernie LaTorre's room.

Dave and the boys ran there, but LaTorre was standing guard.

"Back to class," he said.

But it was too late: The corridor was jammed. No one knew what to do—the PA system was down, too.

"School's canceled," Dave yelled. "Everyone can leave."

"Did they announce it?"

"They can't announce it—there's no electricity."

"Period six. Go back to it," said teacher Ken Lyon.

"Ken, there's something going on in that lav," said Barbara Menard. It sounded like an asylum in there. Someone had shot off a fire extinguisher, and vapor was seeping from under the door. Menard called for help on her walkie-talkie.

"We're burning!" said Dave. He was at the water fountain. "Get your water while you can!"

"Clear the halls," Menard said.

"Uh-oh! Here comes Doc!"

"What are you doing here?" Doc said. "Get in there. What period are you going to? No, you're not. Period six. Go on. Period six." The halls cleared. In a few minutes, the lights came back on.

"Power's on," Dave said. "And only one person got shot!"

Dave could not pass up something as rich with possibility as a power outage, but by year's end, his comedy had evolved. Gone, for the most part, was the pure silliness—walkie-talkies in class, Spam, Dungeons and Dragons in Spanish. Replacing it was humor geared to an older audience—his Radioactive Elvis, his Ed Grimley. In a brainstorming session in World Lit, Dave improvised a skit he called "Dyslexic Kindergarten"; one of its numbers was a takeoff of the kissing song: "Johnny and Janie, sitting in a tree, G-N-I-S-S-I-K!" His classmates howled. For their senior lecture in honors English, Dave, Joel, and Tebow (with the help of Matt Leveille, a junior) wrote about the origins of British comedy. But it wasn't enough to do a paper; they needed a documentary. They prowled Burrillville High with a videocamera, confronting teachers and kids with the question: What do you know about British comedy? Some knew nothing, and their efforts to explain their ignorance were funny. The film ended with Joel expounding on the theory of comedy while, in the background, a person appears to be clubbed to death. Drouin thought they should edit out the flat spots and send it to *Saturday Night Live.* "That's what happens when you are a popular director of wonderful movies," Dave said. "Watch out, Spielberg!"

In his diary, Dave had a mischievous pen. "Today is Passout," he wrote on April 6. "I'm not very good at passing out, but my brother is. Especially after I whack him." Three days later, he wrote: "Good Friday? Aren't all Fridays good? It's the end of the school week and one gets to go out and have fun. I think every Friday is *great* Friday, and the reason why this is *Good* Friday is because religion comes into play. Religion seems to lower the day value."

One night when Beth was over for dinner, the subject turned to the future. Leslie had all but given up hope that the boy who'd once dreamed of becoming an astronaut would ever open a science text again, and she put no stock in an offhand comment Dave had made recently about going into teaching. All she heard about was writing: writing for Drouin, writing in *Godhead,* writing a novel before he turned nineteen. The only other careers that seemed remotely possible anymore were sports broadcasting and comedy.

"I don't care what you do," Leslie said, "I don't care what you are, it doesn't bother me in the least. As long as you are able to support a family and your wife, that's the main thing—and you're happy. But you do have to understand at some point that's going to be your responsibility."

Dave gave Beth a look. *She's being queer again,* it said. Discussion over.

Beth was always at the Bettencourts' now, or so it seemed. She ate there, hung out in Dave's room, sunbathed by the pool, slept over on occasion, even decided to fold clothes one day, an event that bewildered all. ("I just wanted to," Beth explained.) Paul and Leslie had long ago pledged not to intervene in their son's relationship, and they held firm even when Laura announced: "They're planning on getting married, Ma." ("Oh, that's good," Leslie said.)

But Leslie and Paul still had concerns. They worried that Beth would come between Dave and college. They worried about the heart of a fifteen-year-old girl, how love could be so fickle at any age—how their son so easily could be hurt. They were not pleased when Dave gave away hours at Li'l General to have more time for his girl, and as graduation approached, Paul in particular was annoyed that his son was making no effort to find a higher-paying summer job, which would ease next year's tuition bill. Nothing had been handed to Paul and Leslie; what they had they'd earned the old-fashioned way, with hard work.

"Don't worry," Dave said. "Everything's under control."

Changing diapers, midnight feedings, croup—being a parent had seemed so difficult when Dave was an infant, but that was really the easiest part of parenting, wasn't it? Back in Dave's earliest Michael Jordan days, would Leslie ever have believed her son someday would turn to a girlfriend for advice on what to wear? She watched her firstborn, about to leave high school behind—could it be eighteen years since they'd brought him home from the hospital?—and she had a new sense of her own progress through life.

"I can't even imagine what it's going to be like without him around here," she said. "You want to freeze him, say, 'This is nice, you've gone far enough, let's just freeze things for a while.' Because everything's happening so fast."

Paul had another perspective on his son, and it was not one Dave would have expected, considering the friction of late. "I can't think of anything I would want to change other than don't put so many miles on my car!" Paul said. "But really— there's really nothing there that upsets me to the point where I say: 'You've got to change your ways.' He's just a very good, well-rounded kid."

The Sunns saw changes, too.

Beth no longer used so much makeup, no longer did her hair up so big—even mentioned getting it cut. She was still into rings, but most times she wore only Dave's. From Cross Colours, her wardrobe had crept back toward the Gap. That rapper talk had subsided into a diction and vocabulary that hinted of Eastern Establishment. She didn't forsake her beloved street talk entirely, but she had a better sense of when to use it. "You're starting to look like a preppie," Ruth Sunn said, and her daughter did not disagree. Ruth believed one of the profound experiences of her daughter's life was that spring, when Beth happened to witness two boys beating a third at a bus stop near her school. The boy's skull had been fractured and Beth was called to court to testify. "That chastened her quite a bit about violence," Ruth said. "She got to see what really happens."

Even as recently as early spring, screaming matches between mother and daughter had not been uncommon, but now Beth and Ruth laughed at the old flash points, like who got the bathroom first in the morning. Recognizing that someone who had recently turned fifteen might never prevail against someone middle-aged, Beth had made an uneasy peace with her cheerleading adviser. She'd been a *C* student as a sophomore, but now Tim and Ruth listened as she talked of making National Honor Society as a junior, when she'd have to think of college. Beth wanted to attend URI, where Dave would be. She hadn't settled on a career, but she was interested in photography, interior design, and public relations.

Beth's social circle had turned since meeting Dave. The old crew was still in the picture, but with the exception of one close female friend, they'd receded to the background, where Tim and Ruth hoped they would remain. Beth had come between Dave and Joel at first, but the bad feelings had disappeared once Joel started going steady, the previous fall. The rest of Dave's friends and even Dan had allowed Beth into the brotherhood—by June, she had a seat at the Dungeons and Dragons table! If the Sunns had a complaint about the new order, it was that Dave could be so insanely jealous. "Bethany would no more cheat on him or look at another guy or talk on the phone than she would fly to Venus," Ruth said. "I tend to be her severest critic, and I think of all of her best traits, she's true-blue."

Beth and Dave both began to worry about fall, when Dave would be in Kingston, which seemed so far away. Beth had constructed a rosy future in her mind, and it revolved entirely around Dave. He was going to get his degree, she hers, and they were going to marry, move to Vermont, and start a family.

"I want a boy," Beth said.

"That's it?" said Dave.

"A boy and a girl."

"All right."

"I want a boy first, though."

"He'll play basketball," Dave said. "That means he has to have the same middle name as me if he's going to be a junior."

"Yeah—David Paul," Beth said. "The girl's gonna be Victoria Elizabeth Bettencourt, after two of the queens of England. Or maybe Mary Elizabeth."

Dave knew what he'd do with a son.

"I'm going to practice with him since he's three," he said. "He will love basketball!"

"Me and my girl are going to go shopping all the time," Beth said.

"That's good—spend my money!"

"Spend all Dave's money on clothes! And we're going to have a nice house, a big house. A nice big house with a hot tub and a pool and a tennis court. One clay court, 'cause I like clay tennis courts."

"Play-Doh clay."

"And a fountain with a little guy peeing in it," Beth said.

They laughed.

"And a Broadway stage," Beth went on.

"And a moat."

"And a dragon. And little guys on horses who blow their horns every time we leave. I kind of want a horse, but they're kind of too hard to keep good care of."

"We could rent one," Dave suggested.

▲ *Dave at graduation.*

Chapter 15

END OF THE
INNOCENCE

"This class has accrued many honors and is known for its independence."

—STEVE MITCHELL, ON GRADUATION NIGHT

The girl was sobbing to anyone who'd listen. It wasn't fair! It just wasn't fair! So what if her boyfriend had all of a sudden discovered he was academically ineligible for the prom? She had her gown and he had his tux and the limo was rented and the flowers ordered and her mother was letting her have a drinking party afterward and this was the senior prom, which only came once in a lifetime, so why couldn't he go? Why punish her, too, to make some stupid point? And what *was* the point, anyway?

Friday, May 28, the morning of the prom, and the girl was in the corridor outside the principal's office, where her mother was meeting with Chief. If that didn't get them anywhere, Mom was going to the superintendent, and if that failed, well, maybe they would just call *Channel 10 News*! Maybe the girl would go alone and wait until some magical prom moment to take the microphone and make damning statements against them all! "We should just walk out, like in *Beverly Hills 90210*," Heather Gruttadauria said. Make signs and rally the whole senior class and see what they said about that!

Academic ineligibility wasn't the only complication as the last rituals of high school were upon the class of '93. One kid was ripped that his best friend had rented a motel room for him and his girl. Now *that* was antisocial. "He can get laid any night of the week," the friend fumed. "Why tonight?" Another boy had just learned that his date had recently been involved in some sort of free-spirited naked frolic through the woods— with two other girls. Three girls! No guys! Doing—well, who knew what, exactly? Details were scarce, but his source was impeccable and so something must have happened. He didn't care if she were gay, but couldn't she have told him when he'd invited her to the prom? What a long night it was going to be. . . .

And then there was the fiasco over Chad Tupper's party. Chad was one of the easiest-going members of the class of '93, a popular, funny kid who told great stories and shared *Godhead*'s absurdist sensibilities. Since fall, Chad had planned to host a post-prom party. There would be others, but anybody who counted would be at Chad's. Beer would be available, but his parents would be home, and handing over car keys at the door would be the requirement for admission. Kids would pitch tents in the backyard, and at a certain hour the alcohol would be shut off. This was not a novel arrangement; a cheerleader had hosted a similar gathering after the junior prom, without incident. The theory was that kids on prom night would find a way to drink no matter what; better to have them do it where you could keep them from driving.

Not everyone put stock in this theory, well-intentioned as it was. Yesterday, a parent had gotten wind of what was up and called Chad's father to say that if the party went off as advertised, the police would be called. That was it for the alcohol. Chad was willing to proceed, but a few phone calls confirmed that almost no one would come without beer, and so another senior, an in-crowd kid, asked his mother if she would chaperone a drinking party. She agreed. On Friday morning, as word spread that Chad's party was canceled, nobody could believe it. Chad's party had been an item of faith throughout the year! Seniors scrambled to get invited to the other boy's party. On the morning of the senior prom, there was an awful lot of sucking-up going on at Burrillville High.

"So far," Leslie Bettencourt said to her son, "your plans are pretty shaky. I'm not happy. This 'we're going to travel from one party to another' . . . "

The truth was, Dave was clueless about what he was doing after the prom. Not that he much cared right now, standing in the kitchen with his parents making such a fuss over him you'd think they were sending him off to war. In fifteen minutes, Dave had to leave for Beth's, and still his tux didn't look right. It fit the way all formal attire did on him. It created the impression of a scarecrow.

"You're poking my Adam's apple!" Dave said. He felt his throat. That drew attention to what had appeared this week on his chin: the beginnings of his first beard.

"You didn't shave?" his mother said.

"Not that. I'm leaving that."

"God . . . "

"That's as tight as it's going to go back there," said Paul, who was working on Dave's cummerbund. "We should get a child size."

"You're helping a lot, Paul," Leslie said. She moved her husband aside. "Is that better?" she said.

"Looser," Dave said.

"Jesus! Would you take the jacket off for a minute, 'cause I'm working in here . . . hold this . . . that should do it . . . button the coat . . . stand up straight . . . shoulders back."

"Did you get yourself a flower?" Paul said.

Dave said he had a boutonniere. Together with the prom tickets, tuxedo rental, his share of the limo, and Beth's flowers, he'd spent almost two hundred dollars from his Li'l General earnings and his parents on tonight. Beth had spent three hundred—all from Ruth and Tim—on a gown, shoes, handbag, bracelet, earrings, manicure, and hairstyle. She'd also been to a tanning salon. ("I don't care about cancer," she told her diary. "I only go, like, four times to get a base tan, anyway.")

"Do you want me to put it on?" Leslie asked.

"Beth has to do it," Dave said. "And if she fails, Beth's mom has to do it."

"Why can't I do it?"

"Because it's some prom rule or something. I don't know what the hell it is. Do you want to do it?"

"No, it's OK."

Dave was ready.

"Will you get your money and everything else," Paul said, "'cause you're going to walk out forgetting everything and then you'll be screwed."

"I can't find my wallet," Dave said.

"It's in the car," Leslie said.

That was good for one of Dad's mini-lectures.

"Do you want a camera?" Paul said.

"For what do I need a camera, Dad? Hello? They take pictures."

"You should have shaved, you know," Leslie said.

"This is my thinking beard."

"Oh, good," Paul said.

"Get used to it. 'Cause when I'm in college, I'm not going to shave at all."

—

Dave drove to the Sunns'. His parents followed.

"This is it," Ruth said, joshing her daughter. "The night of your life!"

"I love the color of that dress," Leslie said.

"Hold the flowers pretty, honey," Ruth said as relatives took pictures. "That's good."

"Now, they're sleeping over at your house, right?" Leslie said.

"Yeah," said Ruth.

"No, they're not," Tim said.

"They're sleeping at my house? They told me they were sleeping at your house, they told you they were sleeping at my house, so where are they sleeping?"

Dave said his house.

"What time did you say?" Ruth asked.

"Is three reasonable?" Tim said.

"David, what time are you coming in?" Leslie said. "At three?"

"Round about there."

"And you're going to whose house in between?"

Dave mentioned a couple of parties.

"There's no drinking at those places, is there?" asked Ruth. No one answered her.

"If you guys want to come back to our house, you can come back earlier," Leslie said. "We'll make sure we pick up some snacks."

Ruth kissed her daughter and said: "Good-bye. I love you. Have a good time."

"Bye."

"Bye, Dad. Bye, Mom."

"Be good," Leslie said.

Eight were as many as could fit in a limo, and for $495, Dave, Michaelman, Gene, and Brian had rented one. On the way to the prom, they stopped at the mall, where they ate at McDonald's and made a sweep through the All for a Dollar store. Dave picked up a plastic bow-and-arrow set and a Hula Hoop, Brian a pair of garden gloves, Gene a pink lunchbox. "Any mirrors?" Beth said. "We should do this more often," Brian said, "just rent tuxes and come to the mall!"

The prom was at the country club where Paul and Leslie's wedding reception had been, twenty-three years before. It was a heavily chaperoned affair, alcohol-free, with all the soda you could drink. Two seniors who'd had babies over the year came, and one was named a princess; the administration had surrendered to the girl and her academically ineligible boyfriend and allowed them to attend. But another girl, due that summer and starting to show, stayed home. Doc and Chief were there, along with many of the faculty. Ruth and Drouin, old colleagues, spent much of the evening talking shop and remarking how unbelievably grown-up all the girls looked. It was true. The boys looked sophisticated, but it was the girls who seemed to have traveled through some high-fashion zone and emerged ready for the cover of a magazine. It was hard to believe these were the same kids who eight hours ago had been sunbathing in the quad in T-shirts and shorts, until you remembered most had started planning for tonight not long after New Year's Eve.

Ernie LaTorre did the portraits, and Dave posed twice: alone with Beth, and together with Dawes and the *Godhead*-ers. Dave and Beth kissed on the deck at sunset. The deejay played rap, slow music, the Electric Slide, a disco tune, and the infamous Chicken Dance, which kids in Burrillville are introduced to at their first mother-son and father-daughter dances. Drouin and her World Lit students danced while chatting about the fun they would have at the fifth reunion. One good-natured but overweight boy took the floor for a mock

striptease, and for the first time in high school won applause.
So he put his shirt back on and did it again.

At home, as the Bettencourts had fussed over their son, Paul
had recalled the junior prom—how Dave had been in the
Grand March with another boy, and how Paul had taken such
a ration of shit from a friend. "That was faggy," Paul had said.
"I didn't need that aggravation."

"At least they had the good sense not to vote for him," Leslie
said. "It would have been worse if he had gotten queen!"

But Dave was not to be dissuaded tonight. First he did his
Michael Jackson imitation, with Scott Bridge; it brought huge
applause and this comment from Gene's date: "I think Dave
was the boy in the Pepsi commercial!" At the end of the Grand
March, Michaelman, master of ceremonies, made an an-
nouncement: "And finally, returning for another run at super-
stardom—or whatever—escorted by Dave Bettencourt, Brian
Ross!"

At eleven, it was over. Kids took their souvenirs (mugs for
the boys, wineglasses for the girls), and one by one the limos
disappeared into the cool of the night. Dave's group had time
left on their limo, and at $495, they weren't about to waste a
minute, so they had their chauffeur take them to Taco Bell
(China Pit was closed). Then it was back to Gene's, where
everyone had left their cars. Alcohol notwithstanding, Dave
would have dropped by Chad's, whom he liked, but this other
kid was best buddies with the boy who'd roughed him up after
Godhead 2. And it was an in-crowd party. On the other hand,
a lot of Dave's friends would be there, and relations had improved with in crowders—all that coming together.

Dave decided to skip it. He and Beth went with another
couple to a friend's whose parents and sister were away. At
around four, they were back at the Bettencourts'.

—

The next day of school was the Tuesday after Memorial Day. In World Lit, Krissy Remington went to the board, erased the "1" on the countdown, and wrote a zero.

"Guys," she said, "this is our last day." All that was left was exams.

And autographs. Of all the farewell rituals, none compared with signing yearbooks. How could even the very best writer sum up so much in so few words? Autographing had been going on since the past week, and as the last day wound down, Dave scoured the school for the remaining people on his list. *Godhead*ers wrote about the glory of *Godhead,* and Ferg predicted their collegiate version would be a success. Stacey Rawson recalled the brass unicorn Dave gave her at the carnival and observed that since they'd never officially split, they'd probably marry someday. Marcy Coleman praised Dave as funny, charming, and sweet. "Don't change at all," she wrote. "I regret not having you as a student," Ernie LaTorre wrote. "I suspect you are a kindred spirit."

Dave spent part of the final period playing electronic Monopoly on the *Blueprint* computer, then moved into the corridor, where he staged his final Burrillville High performance of Radioactive Elvis. "It's my last chance to do nothing in the hallways!" he said when Richard Polacek walked by. "Make the most of it," Polacek said. Dave wasn't sure if that was a shot, but it didn't matter anymore.

The final buzzer was minutes away when the sister of Dave's friend stormed up. She'd come home to discover that Dave and Beth had been at her house after the prom. And not just at her house—in her room!

"Tammy's telling everyone you and your girlfriend had sex in my bed!" the friend's sister said.

"You don't know the full story," Dave said.

"That's not cool—the whole school knowing you had sex in my bed!"

Dave was uncharacteristically flustered. "You don't know what you're talking about," he said. *Godhead*ers were gathering.

"You were in my room."

"Yeah, but we weren't having sex."

The girl didn't believe Dave, but now the *Godhead*ers were making off-color jokes. Pretty soon, the girl was laughing, too.

Afternoon announcements were read and the buzzer rang. Dave was in no hurry getting to his locker, and when he finally made it, only a few kids were still around. Dave saw Missy Beauchamp, who was crying so hard she couldn't see the numbers on her lock. Dave opened it for her. He opened his own locker and rummaged through the contents: driveway reflectors, a Taco Bell menu, a NO PARKING JAMESTOWN POLICE sign, his walkie-talkie, and, at the very bottom, his Spanish 3 text.

Dave put the walkie-talkie in his backpack and walked with Joel and Colin Brady, his URI roommate, out of Burrillville High into the warmth of the first day of June.

Matt Stone and Krissy Remington were named athletes of the year at the sports banquet. Privately, Dave had hoped to win the basketball sportsmanship award, but it went to someone else. "Great excitement and great food was found at the athletic banquet on this night," he told his diary. "NOT!" At the senior banquet, run by students, Dave joined in the standing ovation for Doc, and he and his fellow *Godhead*ers received the Anonymous Award. On awards night, run by the school, Dave received a scholarship, a journalism achievement award, and a National Honor Society certificate. But while he'd been sports editor of the yearbook, Mindy Ryan did not give him a yearbook award. He didn't care. He knew the teacher who meant most would miss him terribly.

"Dave Bettencourt is delightfully aware of the power of risk, and the requirement that those who are truly special take the risk of making a difference," Drouin wrote in her scholarship recommendation. She went on to describe *Godhead* and the lessons its editor had learned about leadership, responsibility, and taste. "He dealt effectively with consequences," she continued, "and learned that peer and adult scorn really does have a sting. He demonstrated the courage of conviction as well as the wisdom of knowing when to quit."

Most important, Dave had learned how to heed criticism and make changes accordingly. "I am convinced that Dave will always welcome risks and that he will often be greeted in return by success," Drouin concluded. "I also am convinced that his successes will be made sweeter by a powerful sensitivity to others that I have seen peek around the edges of adolescence in this gifted young man."

On graduation day, Dave slept until ten. He talked on the phone with Beth, watched TV, ran some errands for his dad, and by afternoon was outside shooting hoops against the backboard his grandfather had given him many summers ago. It's going to be cool up there tonight, he thought. He wasn't nervous, only filled with the energy he used to have before games.

"Time to shower," his father said through the kitchen window.

"This is the last time I'll be doing this as a high school student," Dave said, and kept on playing.

"Do you have a shirt?" his father said a little while later.

"Everyone else has showered," his mother said.

"David, you're going to be late."

"Right, Dad."

Dave managed to be ready on time. Driving to the high school, he took the back route, past Joel's house and along tree-lined roads into Harrisville. "When we were kids, Joel and I used to ride our bikes to get Slush Puppies there," he said when he passed Li'l General.

In the high school parking lot, classmates compared attire. Many wore shorts under their gowns, despite having been told not to. Dawes had his bowling shoes. Mortarboards were for manifestos, and Gene had decorated his with toy soldiers, Brian with sunglasses that had guitar picks for eyes. In keeping with the medieval theme of the '93 yearbook, Marcy Coleman had knights and a castle from her brother's Lego set. Among Dave's messages were FAREWELL DROUIN, TG, and lines from "The Road Not Taken." He quoted Terry Gimpell: "Knowledge is life. To stop learning is to begin to die."

Graduation was held inside the skating rink, steamy and getting steamier as people filed onto the concrete, where rented folding chairs had been arranged and a stage with a podium and flowers in plastic urns had been erected. The Burrillville High band played "Pomp and Circumstance," and the graduates marched in.

In his address, Chief gave a history of the class, mentioning Drouin's Literary Arts Festival and many athletic achievements among the highlights. He spoke of the challenges facing young people in the era of E-mail, and then Michaelman took the microphone for the class president's welcome. Before he spoke, Michaelman put an Andre the Giant sticker on the front of the podium, where subsequent speakers, including the superintendent, couldn't see it. But the kids could.

Salutatorian Brandie Bozzi spoke of "the end of the innocence," Marcy Coleman of "our once and future time." Joel's father presented diplomas. When Dave's turn came, he crossed the stage, shook Waterman's hand, and received his. Someone

—it was never determined who—hit the scoreboard buzzer. At first, Dave thought it was the fire alarm.

Then he knew. He thrust his hand into the air.

"Yes!" he shouted.

As he returned to his place, he looked into the crowd and found his family and Beth. With only the slightest nudge of imagination, he saw his grandfather, too.

Papa was cheering.

▲ *Dave and Beth open Dave's locker one last time at*
year's end.

Chapter 16

HUCK

*"It's lovely to live on a raft. We had the sky, up there, all
speckled with stars, and we used to lay on our backs and
look up at them, and discuss whether they was made, or
only just happened."*

—from *The Adventures of Huckleberry Finn*

One day after graduation, Dave set off from his house with
Beth. They crossed Round Top Road, hopped a stone wall,
and went down an embankment into woods. He wanted to
show her the old haunts—the places he and Joel played *Return
of the Jedi* and laser tag, their refuge after bottle-rocket attacks
on neighbors' houses.

"This was, like, the best thing," Dave said as they approached a stream, in which there was an island.

Dave helped his girlfriend across the bridge he and Joel had
built with tree limbs. It was shaky, but it held. "Joel and Dan
fell in one day," Dave recalled. "My dad was wicked pissed because he told us not to go too close to the water's edge."

Dave pointed to a cluster of trees in which tenpenny nails,
rusted and headless now, had been driven. "This was our fort.
This was our lookout. Here's the beach. We used to spend,
like, two hours here every day after school."

Dave pointed east, into thick woods.

"We never ventured too far that way," he said. Even now, he wasn't sure what was in that direction.

Dave and Joel were oriented downstream, toward familiar territory. "Our dream was to build a boat and travel down the river to Round Top Pond," Dave said. "A little raft thing, like Huckleberry Finn."

"Did you ever?" Beth asked.

"No. But we had the design."

▲ *Drouin bids farewell.*

Afterword

What's it like growing up in the nineties? I often wondered as I drove past Burrillville High School. I didn't mean an inner-city coming of age; I knew about that from a year I'd spent on another series for *The Providence Journal-Bulletin*. My curiosity was for suburbia. That's where I'd come of age, twenty years before. What about the small-town kids?

Superintendent Dennis D. Flynn was full of questions when I approached him in June 1991. Did I want to use real names? Yes, and photographs, too. How much time would I spend at his school? Just about every day for an entire year. Would I be talking to families? Yes—in fact, what I had in mind wouldn't work unless I got into homes and after-school social circles on a regular basis. I explained that I did not want to write the latest "exclusive!" inside look at a high school, but a portrait of something timeless: the road one travels from child to adult. That summer, I submitted a proposal, which Dennis ran past a lawyer and presented to the school committee with a recommendation to approve. They did.

I met with principal Steve Mitchell in December, and in February 1992, armed with a floor plan of the school, a faculty list, and the names of a handful of students Steve and his secretary, Sheila Jenness, thought I should meet, I was let loose. No one had been told I was coming—the idea was for everyone to be themselves, not on their best behavior—and for a spell, the rumors flew, even though I introduced myself and explained what I was doing everywhere I went. *He's a narc. He's a new teacher. He's Matt Stone's father!* Eventually, word got out. Once it did, I was welcomed everywhere.

As I got to know more and more teachers and kids, I was looking toward September, when the class of '93 would begin its senior year. Before then, I wanted to have the kids I would follow onboard, and parental permission secured. By July, I had chosen five kids from a variety of economic and family backgrounds (a sixth joined us in December). They and many others are in this book, and all have something to say about being an adolescent in the nineties. But for my central character, I went with Dave Bettencourt.

I first noticed Dave at his junior prom, when he lampooned the Grand March by participating with another boy, something a number of adult chaperones—not to mention classmates—did not think was amusing in the least. I considered it a wonderfully irreverent performance in the spirit of Monty Python. My instincts told me that by the end of his senior year, Dave would be someplace quite different from where he was then, in the spring of 1992. When I met Beth Sunn, I was sold. Like most of her peers, Beth was into fads, but unlike many of them, she was strong-willed and independent—more than a match for her boyfriend, who was no slouch when it came to presence. Socializing was paramount now, but looking beyond adolescence, I saw all sorts of marvelous possibilities in Beth. She was, and would continue to be, someone.

Late one night that August, I found myself watching a horror movie with Dave and six other kids in my living room. As my wife and two daughters tried to sleep upstairs, we whooped and hollered and generally carried on, and it was then that I knew the thing was going to work—that these guys would give it to me straight. (The movie, by the way, was the cult classic *Evil Dead II,* though I still say *Evil Dead I* is better.)

Nothing was off-limits with Dave and his friends, so naturally I took advantage. During the course of the year, I went to malls, McDonald's, parties, *Godhead* meetings. I rode with kids in their cars and with Broncos on the team bus. I talked constantly on the phone with my new friends and discovered an appreciation for rap. I spent enough time at Dave's house that I was sure his father was going to have me taking out the trash. Dave and Beth spent enough time at my house that their friends just automatically called here to find out what was going on. I went shopping with Beth and Ruth Sunn. I played Dungeons and Dragons and computer games, had a permanent seat at Dave's lunch table, and went to Friday-night dances, semi-formals, and three proms. I was dragged before the entire school body for the pie-eating contest the day before Thanksgiving (I lost). I was the subject of articles in the school paper and the yearbook, and I wrote a farewell essay for the paper's graduation issue. And of course, I was in class virtually every day. At year's end, Mary Lee Drouin and her World Lit kids dressed me in a cap and gown and, after marching me down the hall, presented me with a diploma.

I was often asked: How do you get along in the world of kids?

My answer always was: perfectly fine, and not just because I finally had an excuse to watch horror movies. I discovered what every veteran teacher told me: Being with kids rejuvenates. The grown-up world has many cynics, but you find few of those at seventeen; most kids that age abound in energy, optimism, and refreshing flakiness, which made my year so interesting. Not that I let myself go. I survived, and ultimately was embraced, because I never hid what I was: an adult writing a book. I did not dress or talk like a teen, or try in any other way to be cool. I was candid about myself, and got candor in return; I was honest, and had honesty returned. I laughed a lot. In the end, that counted the most.

I also was often asked: What's different about growing up today? Is it more difficult?

Sexual mores are different; you need only read the latest survey to know that more kids are having sex, and at an earlier age. Microchips are different. The Information Age, little older than Dave, has brought cable TV, VCRs, home computers, modems, on-line services, and video games, giving today's kids more stimulation and choices than any earlier generation. Spirituality, whether from organized religion or somewhere else, has lost ground to materialism. Violence is so pervasive that even kids not directly harmed are affected by it, in ways we do not fully understand. And it goes without saying that children who are abused, addicted, or from dysfunctional families—and statistics tell us there are more of them than before—face enormous difficulties.

So my answer is: Yes, it is more difficult to grow up today than when I did.

Still, the fundamental issues of adolescence are unchanged. The struggles for identity, individuality, and self-esteem—such horrid buzzwords!—are the same as ever. So is the key to success: an environment in which kids can safely take risks and are encouraged to never stop learning, as Terry Gimpell noted—the kind of environment Chief, Drouin, Paul and Leslie Bettencourt, and many others, gave to Dave.

I got a yearbook, of course, and in the autographing frenzy at year's end, forty-nine kids signed it, nearly a third of the class of '93. Many were kids I spent time with for no other reason than that I liked them, and they me. Being almost forty, I often was asked for advice, which I gladly gave. While my new friends may have thought a writer had a thing or two to say to them, in the end, the lessons were mine. Every day, I was reminded of the potential of youth, even in an age when it's fashionable to believe the young are hopelessly jaded. I learned anew about friendship, the importance of fun, the excitement of secrets, and the power of imagination.

The very best stuff, which all has to do with dreams.

Dave began his yearbook inscription to me with a story. "As the end of our school life ends," he wrote, "a journalist and photographer stand in the hallway. The shining light blinds all that attempt to look at them. Suddenly, the floor begins to rumble and a large, gaping hole opens. The head of a terrible monster peeks out of the hole and swallows the photo man in one gulp. The journalist takes out his red Flair pen gun and fires at the hideous creature. In pain, the evil being bellows loudly, and goes back to its hell home . . . Good story intro, isn't it?"

Dave continued with a bit of nostalgia and then he was at the end of the page. "I will visit you often from college, if that's OK with you," he finished. "Maybe I will become like an uncle to your new child. Or all of your children, since you will have quintuplets! Make sure to read all of my fantasy books in the future. Terry Gimpell lives! *Total Godhead* rules! I'll talk to you later. Love, Dave."

G. Wayne Miller
October 1994
Pascoag, Rhode Island

Acknowledgments

Letting a writer poke around in your life requires extraordinary faith, and I am grateful to those who had it. I never would have gotten anywhere without the unconditional cooperation of Dave Bettencourt, Beth Sunn, and their families; they were invariably polite, understanding, and honest.

My deepest gratitude to Mary Lee Drouin, John Wignot, and Steve Mitchell, who embraced me and my project with an enthusiasm that is a journalist's dream.

My appreciation to those who helped get things off the ground: Bill Eccleston, Barbara Menard, Dennis Flynn, and members of the school committee, especially Alan Chuman and Jack Carroll, refreshing voices of reason and sanity in a sometimes crazy enterprise, town government. Thanks to Mike Menard, Matt Stone, and Lee Malbon.

Thanks to Dawn Glasberg, who maintained a rare equanimity during the slow loss of her mother to cancer.

Thanks to all the teachers at Burrillville High, but especially those who welcomed me into their classrooms, starting with Dick Martin. Nancy Villatico is like Drouin: a teacher who puts her heart and soul into her work. Richard Toomey and

Matt Robinson were wonderful to spend time with, as was Mindy Ryan, whose no-nonsense approach to education is just what some kids need. Thanks also to: Ernie LaTorre, Ken Lyon, Lisa Newman, Jeannine Phelan, Bill Pichie, Andy Auld, Ed Wilk, Tom Gledhill, Roger Hall, Christine Pascarella, Richard Polacek, Gene Kenney, Maria Flanagan, Mary Labossiere, Debra Simone, Moira Cameron, Tony Grello, Dalen Favali, Richard Lapointe, Ron Brissette, Roger Chauvette, Janet McLinden, Peter McLaughlin, Kathryn Liptak, William Griffin. Thanks to administrative aides and assistants, including Diane Carlton, Beverly Hill, Bonnie Kistler, Gloria Tyler, Barbara Brierley, and Sheila Jenness, my first guide to Burrillville High.

Lou Bleiweis, longtime Woonsocket *Call* journalist, helped me with information on Austin T. Levy, his friend. Guidance came from two people at Brown University: Ted Sizer and Fayneese S. Miller, associate professor of education and human development. Two experts with the Rhode Island Department of Health helped: Marcia Campbell and Francis A. Donahue.

The best sources for a small town's history are the local experts, and I had help from three: Pam Cardin of the Burrillville Historical and Preservation Society, and Marshall Shaw and Millie Legg, trusted neighbors and friends.

Kay McCauley has been my agent now for almost nine years, and it's no lie when I say that without her, I'd be just another wannabe. Jon Karp hasn't been my editor for quite as long, but Jon's brilliance and unflagging support have been my salvation. My brother-in-law, Duke Wright, was my gracious host during a long weekend of editing. Thanks also to my sister, Lynda Miller.

Once again, I couldn't have pulled it off without my wife, Alexis, and my colleagues at *The Providence Journal-Bulletin*.

Thanks to my publisher, Steve Hamblett; editors Joel Rawson and Jim Wyman; and writers Brian Jones, Tom Mooney, and Bill Reynolds, as fine a bunch of guys as you're likely to find anywhere. Carol Young edited the series that became the book, and her direction was always on the money. Thanks to copy editor Mark Divver, photographer Timothy C. Barmann, and my good friend, librarian Linda Henderson.

OK, so now it's starting to sound like an Academy Awards speech, but one more moment and I'm out of here. I spent a year with Burrillville kids—almost two, if you add on time before and after the two semesters I was in full-time residence at Burrillville High—and we shared a lot of laughs and secrets. Many kids who didn't make it into this book gave of themselves. I came away confident that, thanks to youth, the future is bright, no matter what the cynics say.

To the class of '93, *carpe diem*!

Resources

Besides hanging out, my most valuable research tool, I went to many places to learn about adolescents today, including regularly to my own *Providence Journal-Bulletin* and *The New York Times.* I read *Young & Modern, Teen,* and *Seventeen,* and eavesdropped on Compuserve's Teen Forum, an electronic bulletin board. I tracked local events in northern Rhode Island through the Woonsocket *Call* and found *The 21st Century: A Journal Written by the Next Generation,* published monthly in Massachusetts and distributed throughout New England, to be particularly helpful.

For further insight into Dave Bettencourt's generation, I read:

Bezilla, Robert, ed. *America's Youth in the 1990s.* Princeton, NJ: The George H. Gallup International Institute, 1993.

Bissinger, H. G. *Friday Night Lights: A Town, a Team, and a Dream.* New York: HarperPerennial, 1991 edition.

Cooper, Karen. *Rhode Island Public Schools: 1992 Education Indicators.* Providence: Rhode Island Department of Elementary & Secondary Education, 1993.

French, Thomas. *South of Heaven: Welcome to High School at the End of the Twentieth Century.* New York: Doubleday, 1993.

Howe, Neil, and Bill Strauss. *13th Gen: Abort, Retry, Ignore, Fail?* New York: Vintage, 1993.

Josephson, Michael. *Ethical Values, Attitudes and Behaviors in American Schools.* Marina del Rey, CA: Josephson Institute of Ethics: 1992.

Just the Facts: A Summary of Recent Information on America's Children and Their Families. National Commission on Children. Washington, DC, 1993.

Speaking of Kids: A National Survey of Children and Parents. National Commission on Children. Washington, DC, 1991.

For insights into contemporary education and adolescent development, I read:

Freedman, Samuel G. *Small Victories: The Real World of a Teacher, Her Students and Their High School.* New York: HarperCollins, 1991.

Kidder, Tracy. *Among Schoolchildren.* Boston: Houghton Mifflin, 1989.

Rose, Peter I., Penina M. Glazer, and Myron Peretz Glazer. *Sociology: Understanding Society.* Needham Heights, MA: Prentice Hall, 1990.

Santrock, John W. *Adolescence.* Dubuque, IA: Wm. C. Brown, fourth edition, 1990.

Saphier, Jon, and Robert Gower. *The Skillful Teacher: Building Your Teaching Skills.* Carlisle, MA: Research for Better Teaching, 1987.

Sizer, Theodore R. *Horace's Compromise: The Dilemma of the American High School.* Boston: Houghton Mifflin, 1992 edition.

———. *Horace's School: Redesigning the American High School.* Boston: Houghton Mifflin, 1992.

Many studies of adolescent behaviors were helpful, including:

Centers for Disease Control and Prevention. "Selected Behaviors That Increase Risk for HIV Infection, Other Sexually Transmitted Diseases, and Unintended Pregnancy Among High School Students— United States, 1991." *Morbidity and Mortality Weekly Report,* v. 41, no. 50, December 18, 1992.

Office of Health Promotion, Rhode Island Department of Health. "Adolescent Substance Abuse Survey." 1992.

Rubenstein, Carin. "Generation Sex: The *Details/Mademoiselle* Report." *Details,* June 1993.

For the impact of violence on America's youth, there is no better book than:

Kotlowitz, Alex. *There Are No Children Here: The Story of Two Boys Growing Up in the Other America.* New York: Anchor, 1991.

For an examination of black inner-city street culture, much of which has been adopted by white suburbia, I recommend:

Donaldson, Greg. *The Ville: Cops & Kids in Urban America.* New York: Ticknor & Fields, 1993.

For background on Burrillville, I read:

Bleiweis, Louis. *Austin T. Levy.* Cambridge: Riverside Press, 1953.

Keach, Horace A. *Burrillville: As It Was, and As It Is.* Providence: Knowles, Anthony, 1856.

Mehrtens, Patricia A. *One Hundred Years Ago in Burrillville: Selected Stories from the Local Newspapers.* Bowie, MD: Heritage Books, 1992.

Nebiker, Walter. *Historic and Architectural Resources of Burrillville, Rhode Island: A Preliminary Report.* Providence: Rhode Island Historical Preservation Commission, 1982.

And I found a documentary film useful:

Billington, Robert, producer and director. *The Fiber That Wove America's Spirit: The Blackstone River Valley of Rhode Island.* Cumberland, RI: Blackstone Valley Tourism Council, 1989.

For background on Maine Indians, two publications were helpful:

Penobscot Indian Nation. *Maine Indians: A Brief Summary.* Old Town, ME, 1983.

Scully, Diane. *Maine Indian Claims Settlement: Concepts, Context and Perspectives.* Augusta, ME: Maine Indian Tribal-State Commission, draft, 1993.

ABOUT THE AUTHOR

G. WAYNE MILLER is a staff writer at *The Providence Journal-Bulletin*. A Harvard graduate, he lives in Pascoag, Rhode Island, with his wife and three children. He is at work on a book about marketing and children's culture.

ABOUT THE TYPE

This book was set in Garamond, a typeface originally designed by the Parisian type cutter Claude Garamond (1480–1561). This version of Garamond was modeled on a 1592 specimen sheet from the Egenolff-Berner foundry, which was produced from types assumed to have been brought to Frankfurt by the punch cutter Jacques Sabon (d. 1580).

Claude Garamond's distinguished romans and italics first appeared in *Opera Ciceronis* in 1543–44. The Garamond types are clear, open, and elegant.